Through Thick and Thin

Teens Write About Obesity, Eating Disorders, and Self-Image

By Youth Communication

Edited by Hope Vanderberg

Through Thick and Thin

EXECUTIVE EDITORS
Keith Hefner and Laura Longhine

CONTRIBUTING EDITORS
Kendra Hurley, Andrea Estepa, Clarence Haynes, Laura Longhine,
Tamar Rothenberg, Rachel Blustain, Al Desetta, Katia Hetter,
Philip Kay, Nora McCarthy, and Hope Vanderberg

LAYOUT & DESIGN
Efrain Reyes, Jr. and Jeff Faerber

COVER ART
Elizabeth Deegan

Copyright © 2009 by Youth Communication®

All rights reserved under International and Pan-American Copyright Conventions. Unless otherwise noted, no part of this book may be reproduced, stored in a retrieval system, or transmitted in any form or by any means, electronic, mechanical, photocopying, recording, or otherwise, without express written permission of the publisher, except for brief quotations or critical reviews.

For reprint information, please contact Youth Communication.

ISBN 978-1-933939-93-3

Second, Expanded Edition
The first edition of this book was entitled *I Took Dieting Too Far*.

Printed in the United States of America

Youth Communication®
New York, New York
www.youthcomm.org

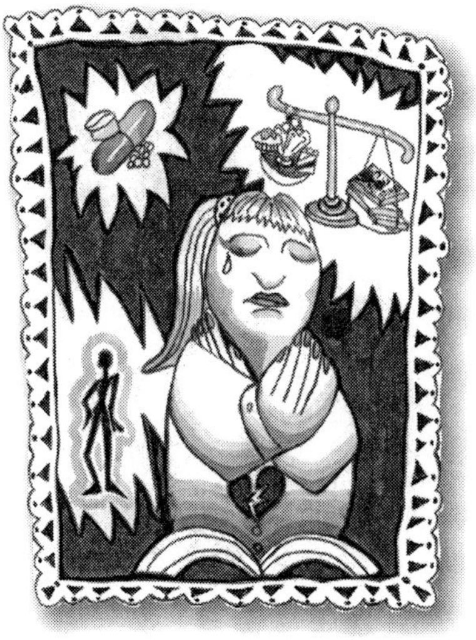

Table of Contents

Addicted to Food, *Miguel Ayala* 13
    Miguel feels powerless to control his eating.

Lighten Up on Heavy People, *Jennifer Cuttino* 16
    Jennifer has been teased and insulted about her size for years.

Scaling Back, *Erica Harrigan* 20
    Erica grew up using food to calm herself, but feels stronger when she gets her eating habits under control.

Shapin' Up!, *Antwaun Garcia* 24
    When Antwaun balloons up to 291 pounds, he makes a plan to get back in shape.

My Body Betrayed Me, *Christine M.* 28
    After years of childhood abuse, Christine doesn't know how to have a healthy relationship with her body.

Big, Black, and Beautiful, *Anonymous* 32
    As a black girl at a mostly white school, the writer gets mixed messages about what's beautiful.

How I Overcame Being Overweight, *Shaniqua Sockwell* 37
    Shaniqua struggles to find a weight that's right for her.

Are Teens Getting Too Fat?, *Megan Cohen* 41
    Megan interviews a doctor about the effects of obesity among teens.

Contents

The War of the Weights, *Elizabeth Thompson* 45
   Elizabeth wishes girls would stop commenting on each other's size.

Naturally Thin, *Desirée Guéry* 49
   Desirée is very thin, and has to deal with constant comments about her weight.

Overboard With Exercise, *Shavone Harris* 54
   Shavone takes up strenuous physical exercise to lose weight and be accepted by her peers.

I Took Dieting Too Far, *Renu George* 59
   Tired of being teased about being "chubby," Renu starts eating less, and soon becomes obsessed with losing weight.

What Are Eating Disorders?, *Stephanie Perez* 66
   A psychologist explains anorexia and bulimia.

Starving for Acceptance, *Anonymous* 68
   Striving to look like the skinny girls in her school, the writer embarks on dangerous periods of restricting her food.

Male on the Scale, *Anonymous* 74
   The writer describes his struggles with eating disorders.

Contents

My Secret Habit, *Anonymous* 77
   The writer starts throwing up her food to lose weight, but stops when a friend is hospitalized for bulimia.

Traumatized By Eating, *Autumn Bush* 82
   Refusing to eat becomes a way for Autumn to escape her problems.

Skinniest Man in the Graveyard, *Anonymous* 88
   As a teen, the male writer becomes obsessed with shedding pounds and resorts to anorexia and bulimia.

Sticks and Stones, *Anne Ueland* 94
   Anne is ridiculed by her mother and her peers because of her weight. She longs to be comfortable with who she is and the way she looks.

Finding My Way Home, *Aquellah Mahdi* 98
   After years of living with an eating disorder, Aquellah enters a treatment center and begins the slow process of recovery.

Recovering From an Eating Disorder 105
   A therapist explains what causes eating disorders and how you can recover.

FICTION SPECIAL: Lost and Found, *Anne Schraff* 111

Teens: How to Get More Out of This Book 118

How to Use This Book in Staff Training 119

Contents

Teachers and Staff: How to Use This Book In Groups 120

Credits 122

About Youth Communication 123

About the Editors 126

More Helpful Books from Youth Communication 128

Introduction

"Food is either my best friend or my worst enemy," writes Miguel Ayala in his story, "Addicted to Food." Growing up in a house where there often wasn't enough to eat, he learned to associate being full with being happy and in control of his life. But now, he writes, he can't seem to control his addiction to eating.

For the teen writers in this book, the old saying "you are what you eat" takes on a whole new meaning. Whether they're struggling with overeating or with eating disorders like anorexia and bulimia, their uneasy relationship with food and weight often reflects how they feel about themselves.

Some writers have learned to overcome their overeating habits. A girl's comment about Antwaun Garcia's weight gives him the initial push to start working out and eating healthier. To his surprise, he finds that setting a goal and accomplishing it is as satisfying as the weight loss.

Other writers explore diets and weight loss programs that work for them, while some end up taking it too far. In "Overboard With Exercise," Shavone Harris finds that being good at sports gave her a way to fit in as an overweight child. But years later, her fear of gaining weight and being ostracized leads her to become obsessed with exercising.

But for the majority of the teens in this book—male and female—an obsession with weight and control takes the form of eating disorders like anorexia and bulimia. Many of these writers are also in foster care and have suffered from various forms of abuse at home.

This is no coincidence. Eating disorders are often a way to cope with trauma. "An eating disorder keeps you so preoccupied that it helps you avoid remembering stuff from your past that's traumatic," says therapist Mary Hopper in "Recovering From an Eating Disorder." She explains that manipulating food and weight also offers a distraction from the things these teens can't control in their lives, and helps them numb to their pain.

In her story, "Traumatized By Eating," Autumn Bush explains it well: "Instead of worrying about the problems I couldn't control, I could just worry about what I had or hadn't eaten that day," she writes. Eventually she finds a foster mother who helps her make the first steps toward recovery.

Aquellah Mahdi found that denying herself food gave her a sense of control. She couldn't stop the abuse she was experiencing, but "I was in charge of what went into my body and how it was going to come out," she writes in "Finding My Way Home." She eventually seeks treatment at The Renfrew Center, an inpatient eating disorder clinic. There, she learns how to say goodbye to her eating disorder and for the first time sees the possibility that she can beat her disease for good.

For readers who have struggled with their own eating issues, the stories in this book offer hope that you can develop a healthier relationship with what you eat, and learn to love who you are.

In some of the stories, names and identifying details have been changed.

Addicted to Food

By Miguel Ayala

Ever since I was little I've used food to comfort myself. I stuff myself with food to help me sleep. I have an attack of the munchies whenever my emotions feel out of control (which is often). Right now I'm thinking of getting a hot chocolate and cookies to satisfy my sadness. And it would work. When I'm full I feel a lot better.

I love cereal, Chinese food, pizza, chicken, and hamburgers. I find chocolate irresistible. Food is either my best friend or my worst enemy. If I enjoy what I'm eating I feel happy. If I don't have enough to eat I feel unhappy.

But eating the way I do has its problems. Sometimes I can't stop eating. I just want to eat more and more. Then I feel bad about myself and embarrassed. I'm getting bigger and bigger. I can't fit into clothes I bought six months ago and I can't walk up stairs without feeling winded.

My mom used food to punish me and reward me. If I did something wrong, like skip my homework, she would make me eat liver and onions over rice. So whenever she made liver for dinner I knew I was in the "danger zone" with her, and I would be extra careful to do whatever she wanted.

But when my mom was in a good mood, she would reward us with food we all liked, like a ham and egg sandwich. When she served eggs I would let my guard down slightly and feel more mellow.

Now I sometimes reward myself with food. I'll tell myself, "If I do everything right today I will buy some Chinese food."

Everything felt happier in our house when we had food, so I started to imagine that eating was what made things better.

Sometimes when I was little we had no food and had to eat leftovers for two or three days. Other times we had to use the New York City summer feeding program to eat, and we'd go from one school to another for food. It depressed and embarrassed me to think we couldn't eat because we had no money.

But when we had food, it felt good. We could open the refrigerator and eat.

Soon I was eating more and more whenever we did have food. Part of it was because I felt like we should eat a lot when we had food, since I went hungry so much of the time. But partly it was that everything felt happier in our house when we had food, so I started to imagine that eating was what made things better.

I started to realize my eating was a problem when people started saying, "Miguel! You're getting fat!" They were right. I noticed my clothes feeling smaller. But I didn't know how to stop eating when I felt bad and food was around. I still don't.

I'm getting scared about my weight. Sometimes I have a hard time keeping my balance, and when I sit down it sounds like I punched the wall. You can read in the papers about men who die of heart attacks or high cholesterol or diabetes because they're too big. On top of that, people in my group home (I'm in foster care now) are always calling me "fat f-ck," and I hate that.

Still, when I am sad and depressed, all I want to do is eat. It gets really out of control when I eat something I find delicious. Then I just want more and more. Whenever I feel hungry, I start remembering living with my mother. I see visions of my past, starving for hours, and I feel worse and want food to feel better again.

Residents at my group home say things like, "Stop eating so much and maybe you could lose some weight." I know they say this to help, but it makes me feel embarrassed and inferior. I know they're right—I have to quit eating so much, but I just can't. I feel addicted to food.

Miguel was 20 when he wrote this story.

Lighten Up on Heavy People

By Jennifer Cuttino

There are many different types of prejudices—some people make judgments based on race, nationality, religion, and even appearance. I have been the victim of prejudice because I'm overweight.

I am 18 years old and weigh over 200 lbs. I've had a weight problem most of my life. I really started to gain weight in elementary school. At lunchtime, I ate my lunch and picked off the plates of other students who couldn't finish their lunch. I did the same thing at home, especially at Thanksgiving and Christmas when my relatives were too stuffed to eat anymore. And when anyone called for seconds, I was always the first in line.

Dealing with my weight problem in elementary school wasn't that hard. I wasn't teased too much because I was still young and I wasn't that heavy yet. But when I was in junior high, I was teased everyday—mostly by people I knew. One boy named

Taheed would say things like, "Hey, hey, hey, it's Fat Jennifer," or, "It's two tons of fun." He would laugh out loud and so would the rest of the class.

My weight was always the target of someone's joke. They would expect me to excuse them when they said, "You know I'm just playing with you." But I think that deep down they really meant it and didn't care about my feelings.

In high school I had the worst time. If there was a group of boys standing together when I walked in the halls, one of them would say, "Yo, there goes yours right there," or "Hey! My friend right here wants to talk to you." I would pretend to ignore them and just keep on walking, but inside I was both hurt and embarrassed.

One day in my freshman year of high school, I got on the student elevator and went to the back. It was crowded and everyone was squeezed together. The doors wouldn't close and people started getting angry because they were late to class. Then someone yelled, "We're over capacity, throw all the fat bitches out!"

At that moment everyone in the elevator turned around and looked at me. I felt like just curling up in that corner and dying. Luckily the elevator doors closed and took us up to the top floor. When everyone got out, I had to force myself to go to class. I felt like crying.

Gym class was always a problem. I failed gym because I didn't want to get dressed or participate. I felt self-conscious seeing everyone else in their shorts or gym uniform while I was in my jogging pants.

I often feel embarrassed going about my day-to-day life even when I'm not in school. When I get on the bus or the subway I try to sit in a single seat because in a double seat I take up one and a quarter seats. When people get on the bus, I can feel the hostile stares—they look at me as if to say, "You're so big you take up the whole damn seat."

I don't go to parties with my friends because I feel out of place. If I do go to a party, I just sit in the corner and watch everyone else dance and have a good time.

Luckily, I've always had some good friends who have stood behind me. When someone teased me in school, my friend Kerri would always go up to them and defend me because she didn't like anyone bothering me. All of my friends have been on my side. They have accepted me for the person I am. They sometimes talk to me about doing something about my weight problem because they care about me and know how cruel and insensitive people can be.

My family has also been there for me. My mother is very supportive. She's always thinking of diets and ways of helping me deal with my weight problem. She is my best friend in the world and I love her very much for that. My mother worries about my health because I'm so heavy.

> **One boy would say things like, "Hey, hey, hey, it's Fat Jennifer," or, "It's two tons of fun."**

I have to lose weight because I want to be around a long time.

I am now going to NutriSystem Weight Loss Centers. So far, I've lost 50 lbs and I am starting to feel better about myself. They're teaching me about proper nutrition and not only how to lose weight, but how to keep it off.

The program is very personalized. You eat their pre-packaged food and it tastes really good. You go every week to get weighed in and get your weekly supply of food: breakfast, lunch, dinner, dessert, and "craving control snacks" which include popcorn, pretzels, and low-calorie candy bars. You eat them when you feel the munchies coming on.

NutriSystem also has a program called "Behavior Breakthrough." It's basically a group counseling session that involves going to class and talking with other people on the program. We sit at a table and talk about how our week went and how we are doing on the program. I find that talking with people who are in the same boat that I'm in makes it much easier to lose the weight and continue the program.

I can't wait till I get down to my goal weight. When I do, I'm going to go to parties and clubs and buy the nicest clothes. But what I want to do most is go and find all those people who made fun of me all through junior high and high school—the people who said I'd always be fat. I will go up to them and say, "How ya like me now?"

Jennifer was 18 when she wrote this story.

Scaling Back

By Erica Harrigan

When I was 12, eating became a way to soothe myself. That year I was admitted into a mental institution to deal with the anger I had from being abused as a child.

At the mental hospital, I started taking anti-depressants. The medicine helped my moods but made me into a pig—and I was already a big eater. I would eat five times a day: Breakfast, lunch, dinner and two snacks, and I always had seconds at breakfast and thirds at lunch and dinner. (If they hadn't given me a limit, I probably would've had seconds of snacks, too.)

I would eat, then go straight to my room and sleep all day. I slept so much because I felt depressed. Even though I felt safe in the hospital, I wanted to be free. I felt like I was locked up in a cage.

I also isolated myself because if I interacted with the other

Scaling Back

kids, they would drive me to the point of spazzing out and I would misbehave. If one person acted out we all got penalized for it.

If I was doing well and one person acted stupid and ruined everything, I'd just explode and attack whoever stepped out of line. Other times, I was the one who acted up. Then I'd get restrained and medicated.

After two or three months in the hospital, I went from about 70 lbs to 300 lbs. I just blew up. I actually felt good about gaining weight. When I was skinny, people made fun of me, calling me "sacks of bones" and "crack baby." Those names hurt.

I also liked being overweight because I'd been raped when I was 9, and I used to think I was raped because I was sexy. (Later I realized I was just a kid, and that my looks had nothing to do with it.) I believed that being fat would make me unattractive to guys, so I felt safe.

It took a long time for me to realize that, once again, I was hurting myself by letting my body get out of my control

But when I was older, I got moved to a residential treatment center, went off the medication that had made me gain a lot of weight, and dropped 150 lbs.

On weekends I stayed with family in Harlem and hung out with my cousin. My cousin was like a sister or a role model to me. Anything she did I wanted to do. I got my tongue pierced and a nose ring because she did. We went out together to clubs and parties.

My cousin liked to play boys so I tried to do the same. The more I visited my aunt's crib, the more I became hot in the pants. One day, on a dare, I had sex. I didn't like it, but I liked the feeling of being accepted by the boys in my hood. After that I had sex just to be down, and instead of using food to calm myself, I used sex to make myself feel wanted and accepted.

I really didn't enjoy the sex with any guys, because it made me remember my past experiences. But I wanted love, and I thought that was how I could get it. It took a long time for me to come to my senses and realize that, once again, I was hurting myself by letting my body get out of my control.

Truthfully, I needed help to take more control of my body. I couldn't imagine how I could calm myself down without being addicted to food or sex.

My current boyfriend showed me what true love is all about. He told me, "Love isn't just about sex. Sex is only part of the relationship. A relationship is about support, communication, affection, and loyalty."

I started to realize that a guy could like me for myself, not for my body. With his help, I stopped sleeping around. It was hard because sex was a comfort to me, even though it was also scary and depressing.

> *I'd eat like a pig when I was angry and like a garbage truck when I was sad.*

After I calmed down on sex, I noticed that when I was feeling emotional, I'd eat. I'd eat like a pig when I was angry and like a garbage truck when I was sad. When I was lonely, I'd eat 'til my belly was stuffed. After I stuffed myself, I'd feel greedy, like I was a fat slob taking in all the food I could eat. It was almost the same emotions for me as having sex: I'd feel good while I was eating, but afterward I'd feel nasty.

One time my boyfriend left New York for a weekend. I felt lonely. I called him constantly and got no answer. I was worried so I isolated myself and ate half of what was in the refrigerator: hot dogs, sandwiches, cereal. I would have helped myself to the rest but, luckily, I had to think about my roommates. I didn't want them to starve.

A few months ago, though, I decided that if I could take control of my sexuality, I could take control of my eating. I felt scared that I was putting my health at risk. I knew I ate too much fat and junk food and drank a lot of sugary sodas. I wanted to begin taking care of myself better, so I decided to eat healthier foods.

I began to cut down on pork and beef, because they're fattening and can give you high cholesterol. I came up with substitutes like turkey and tuna fish, which are lower in fat.

I ate more vegetables, such as spinach, peas, carrots and corn. (For a while I went overboard on the corn, eating 5-10 cans a week. Then I found out corn has a lot of sugar, so I started to cut back.) I also ate more plums and grapes, apples and oranges, and my favorite fruit, mangos.

At first it was hard to balance my meals. I craved junk food, and felt hungry a lot. But eventually, eating healthy became a habit. I felt proud that I tried to change a way of living that was hurting me and succeeded. Taking control of my sex life and my eating habits makes me feel I'm capable of doing anything.

Since I've been eating healthier, I've had more energy. I've also noticed that I have dropped a few pounds. I didn't mean to be dieting. I felt fine about how I looked and just wanted to be healthier. But I'm glad to know that changing what I eat is having an impact on my body.

The biggest change is that I rarely eat just to eat now. I try to eat only when I'm hungry. I feel healthier and stronger, and my will power is stronger. Most important, I feel my body is much more under my own control.

Erica was 19 when she wrote this story.
She later married and had two children.

Shapin' Up!

By Antwaun Garcia

Before I went into foster care at age 9, I was slim. I was the skinniest of all my cousins. We never had much food in my house, so when I came into my foster home I was straight. At times I couldn't stop eating. I started to gain weight, but I stayed in shape playing basketball.

At the age of 14 I began lifting weights to improve my body. I figured that to be in shape and add a little muscle wouldn't hurt me. So I began lifting about 200 lbs of free weights to build up my chest and my arms.

But when I hit about 15 I stopped playing basketball. I also started drinking nothing but soda and eating twice as much as I did before. Instead of having one sandwich I would have two with extra mayo. When my aunt made chicken I would eat at least a whole chicken myself. I would stay out late eating street food, the usual Chinese food, pizza, beef patties, Oreos and Doritos. I began to gain a whole lot of weight. Between ages 15 and 17, I must have gained about 150 lbs.

I didn't realize how big I was getting until I looked at pictures and saw I had a fat neck. My stomach was out there, and my thighs were as huge as Oprah's in her fat phase. I hated the way I looked, and I noticed I wasn't getting the same response from females as I did when I was slimmer. I knew I needed to think about losing weight.

Then one summer two years ago, I was with a female and she flat out told me that she was not used to dating big men. She said that in some ways she was embarrassed by me.

I knew I had to lose weight but her comments pushed me over the limit. I was like, "It's a wrap. It's time to train like Rocky."

I went to get a routine check up from the doctor and I weighed 291 lbs. I was pissed that I had allowed myself to get that big. The next week I began my training, harder than I ever had in my life.

I had something to prove to myself, and I wouldn't let anyone stop me from losing weight. I was going to lose it the right way, and I knew no diet would work. I wasn't messing with no pills, no drinks and no special impossible-to-follow diet.

I started to drink more water, about five to six glasses a day. I began eating less. I still ate what I would usually eat, the same baked ziti, chicken, all that good stuff. The difference was how much I ate. I knew to eat one piece of chicken instead of the whole bird, eat mainly vegetables and stay away from simple carbohydrates like white bread, rice and potatoes. Instead of sucking down six pieces of Wonder bread, I would eat two pieces of wheat bread.

Before, I never ate breakfast in the morning, so when I came home to eat lunch, I would eat too much. Then I would have a big dinner and fall asleep. I couldn't do that anymore, not if I wanted to lose weight. So I would eat something for breakfast, maybe a banana and some orange juice. When I came home for lunch I wasn't as hungry. So I would eat a tuna sandwich and drink a glass of milk and then have an apple for a snack a half hour later. That way I wouldn't be starving for dinner. At dinnertime I would eat less meat and starch and twice as many veggies. At night if I wanted a snack I ate crackers with a little Kool-Aid. I was good.

I also started working out again. My basic workout was shadow boxing. That's no different from boxing, but it's by yourself. I figured that boxers are some of the fittest athletes around, so why not imitate them to get in shape? I would work on the speed of my jabs and hooks.

After about 15 minutes of boxing, I would do some sit-ups and then some push-ups. I would do no more than about 20 push ups to start off with and about 50 sit-ups a night. I also bought a jump rope to help build my endurance and stamina. I would jump rope for at least three minutes straight.

Instead of sucking down six pieces of Wonder bread, I would eat two pieces of wheat bread.

When I first started, I knew my body wouldn't be able to take long workouts like it used to. I would start off working out for only a half hour. Then, after every month, I planned to increase the time by about 10 to 15 minutes so my body could get adjusted to it. I also knew working out solo would be boring, so I added some music to my routine. Also, I went back to playing basketball.

Sometimes when I trained I thought about that comment my girl said to me, that I was too big for her. Then I would think, "Who cares what she says, this is about my health and if I don't give two f-cks about it, then who will?"

I worked out the whole winter. When Thanksgiving and Christmas came around, I ate whatever I wanted, but that next morning, I worked all the turkey, chicken, and cakes off. From December 12 to the end of February I worked out continually. When March hit, the results of my work were visible. People were like, "Antwaun! Oh my God, you lost so much weight!"

At first I didn't pay no mind to it. I thought they were saying it to say it. Then more and more people told me that I had lost weight. My teachers in my school, my grandparents, my aunt, my cousins, and even the girl who was embarrassed by me. She was all on me, like, "You look so good. I'm so proud of you."

I was thinking, "I didn't do this for you! I did this for myself."

But it was true. I'd lost a lot of weight. I was able to wear tank tops, and they fit me properly. I could fit into my old jerseys and sweaters. When I got back on the scale that March I weighed 240. I had lost 51 lbs in three months. I did all that with no diet, no pills, just a lot of working out and eating properly.

I began wearing brighter colors because I looked right in them. I wore more white, more red, gray and blue. I took pics wherever I went, and I noticed the difference in my appearance.

I still feel I have some weight to lose. Now I am 233-235 lbs, and I am 6'1", so I don't want to lose more than 20-30 lbs. But I think a solid 200-215 lbs would fit me fine. I want to keep in shape, maybe build a little six-pack, and some LL Cool J arms. (I think he has the body every guy wants.)

But for now, I'm also happy with what I've accomplished. It felt good to lose weight, and it felt good to set a goal and stick to it.

Antwaun was 19 when he wrote this story.

My Body Betrayed Me

By Christine M.

I hate this body I live in. It's a waste, an eyesore. I look in the mirror and long for longer legs, more curvaceous hips, a slimmer waist, a longer neck—basically I want everything to change. Almost every night when I'm going to sleep I imagine having the body I've always dreamed of, the body that I believe would make me happy. I know another body probably wouldn't change my feelings, but I can't seem to change the way I feel about this skin I'm in.

Even though I daydream and sleep-dream and pray and hope to have a new and different body, I'm terrified to think of what might become of me if my wish came true. The few times in my life I've exercised, when people started to compliment me on the weight I was losing I freaked out and stopped. Why do I yearn for a body I'll be terrified to have? I think a lot of it has to do with the abuse I suffered as a child.

I don't think there was ever a time in my childhood when I wasn't being abused. In order to survive, I made believe that the real me was separate from my body. That way, the abuse was happening not really to me, but just this skin I'm in.

Still, my body sometimes betrayed me. Crying when I wanted to remain strong, becoming tired and refusing to obey my commands to stay awake, and, most horribly, physically responding to sexual advances. It seemed to me like my body had a mind of its own. I hated the thought of sexual contact, yet my body would respond to it, even when it was unwanted.

My father said that what he was doing to me was caused by something I had done, and I believed him. I tried not to do anything to get him started. I made sure I didn't pout, or sit with my legs open, or bite my pinkie finger (all the things he said made me "ask for it"). But no matter what I did, something would set him off. I blamed my body.

My mother was no better. She was always looking for some excuse to hit me. I couldn't for the life of me figure out what I did to spark that hatred in her. I'm not sure how old I was when I finally started to notice the skin tone difference between my mom, my sister, and me.

My mother and my sister were a lot lighter than I was. I was the only dark-skinned one in my mother's brood. It wasn't too long after that realization hit me that I started to notice how my mom always took her anger out on me and not my sister, who, truth be told, was more of a hellion than I was. "Maybe it's because I'm darker than she is," I thought. This made me hate my skin even more.

I hated everything about myself, including my eating habits. Sometimes I just couldn't stop myself from eating. Even when I was full I couldn't resist having one more chip or one more piece of chicken. Half of the time I wasn't even hungry when I ate. I just wanted something to fill the empty hole inside me.

If my mother and I had a fight, or if I got a bad grade at

school, I would crawl up under the covers with a bag of chips or cookies or whatever I could get my hands on and stuff my face. Afterwards, when my stomach was bulging and my cheeks were sore, I hated myself. "Horrible, ugly pig!" I would scream in my head and I would punch my thighs or methodically bang my head against the wall.

When I entered foster care and the abuse stopped, I had gotten used to feeling like my body didn't belong to me, and that it was more like an enemy that always betrayed me. I no longer felt any attachment to my body at all, just great disgust.

In foster care, I was required to go to therapy, but not required to talk. So I kept these and all my other feelings to myself. Talking about them just seemed too painful and frightening.

Recently, however, I started therapy again, but this time it was because I wanted to, not because I was forced to. Gradually I've started to let down my guard around my therapist and let her in on my worst thoughts and feelings about my body and the things that were said and done to me.

> *I made believe that the real me was separate from my body.*

I was scared that my therapist would agree with me that my body was a hideous thing. I was afraid she would turn away from me in disgust, or worse, agree with the people who told me that me getting abused was my fault. She didn't do this. She sat and listened, not passing judgment, just listening and letting me get it out.

And something strange happened to me as I told her these secret thoughts. I began to see how utterly ridiculous these thoughts were. No way could a child be responsible for the actions of an adult. Whether I acted seductive or not, my father should have known better than to do any of the things he did to me. My mother should have loved me without putting her hands on me no matter what color my skin was. As a child I was responsible for no one's actions but my own.

Of course, knowing this in my mind and accepting it with my heart are two different things. My mind may be able to understand that the abuse I went through as a child wasn't my fault, but my body and my heart can't understand this so readily.

It's still hard for me to look at myself in the mirror without feeling a ripple of disgust. I prefer getting dressed in the dark, and my body still flinches at a person's touch.

It's hard for me to even feel my body sometimes. It's as if I'm watching myself do things with no conscious sense of doing them. It's as though I'm completely separate from my body. Most of the time I feel like I'm floating around, and I am startled to find that I have a body at all. Even now, I'm just watching my hands float across the keyboard, amazed.

I'm trying to become more connected to my body. Sometimes sharp pain brings me back into contact with myself. If I suddenly move my neck when it's stiff, or my foot falls asleep and then awakens (you know that prickly feeling?), I become aware of my body with a quick start.

But I don't know if I'll ever feel connected to my body the way most people are. I like to say that I don't see the point in the connection, but the truth is I'm really terrified of it.

Sometimes in therapy, it's like I can feel the sensations of what happened to me when I was younger. If I became connected to my body, would those feelings I tried to ignore come flooding back? And, if so, could that be my undoing? My therapist said it won't kill me. She says if I survived the abuse I can get through the memories of it. But I'm not so sure.

Pretending that I didn't have a body helped me survive years of abuse. I'm not sure I want to change that now.

Christine was 22 when she wrote this story.

Big, Black, and Beautiful

By Anonymous

It took me a long time to convince myself that I am a beautiful girl.

I grew up going to a private school where I was one of only a few black students. At that school, it seemed like only the thin, blond, and big-chested girls were considered appealing.

I am 5'7" and weigh 150 lbs. I am truly a brick house and have been called thick many times. No matter how fit I was, people regularly commented on my size because I wasn't thin and didn't look like a supermodel.

Some students would talk about my round butt, thick hair and lips and shapely figure. "Nobody wants your fat butt," one guy told me.

I constantly worried about my physical appearance as a result. Whenever I'd get around friends I'd ask, "How does my hair look?" or, "Do I look fat in this outfit?" I was becoming almost annoying.

Because of the comments about my body, I often felt hurt, sad, and angry. Even if my friends and family told me how pretty, smart, or popular I was, the weight slurs would go straight to my head.

I'd try to defend myself, but that would only make them bother me even more. They knew the slurs would hurt me, even if what they said was not true.

I felt so bad about myself that when attractive black guys looked at me, I'd turn my head and look the other way. I thought I knew what they wanted—white girls, Hispanic girls, or light-skinned black girls with long legs and straight hair.

But at the same time, I'd get whistles and catcalls from black and Hispanic guys on the street who said complimentary things about my body. I'd wonder why they bothered. I was the big girl, the fat one.

It hurt the most when the boys would call me fat. Most of the guys in my school were white. The ones who weren't liked white girls, or at least the girls who looked like white girls. And since there weren't many black guys in my school, I wanted to please the white guys and look and act the way they wanted me to.

A great thing about my school was that I could date guys of different races and no one would stare or say a thing, because everybody dated each other. But because I dated white guys, my friends outside of school called me a "white girl." They didn't like that I dated out of my race.

And I felt it was not exactly normal, because when my white boyfriends and I would go out to the movies or the mall, we'd get stares. One time an old boyfriend and I were waiting in the train station. A Hispanic guy started to sing "Jungle Fever," a Stevie Wonder song about interracial couples.

My boyfriend and I just looked at each other and started to laugh. But it wasn't funny. It wasn't anyone's business what we did.

Through Thick and Thin

Even though I tried to look and act like a white girl with my friends from school, when I hung out with friends outside of school I had to try and act cool, maybe even throw in some slang. But I sounded so stupid that I got picked on even more.

I was always called the "white girl" whenever I was around my family or my black friends who didn't go to my school.

"Do you think you have thin lips?" or "Why do you fling your hair like that?" they would ask.

I'd try to ignore their comments, which were about everything from my legs to my hair. But it was hard.

Once, when a friend noticed I was shaving my legs, she looked at me disapprovingly and said, "Black girls don't shave their legs!"

I asked her what she meant by that and she said, "Black guys think hairy legs are sexy." I don't think that's always true, or that it even matters.

My friend also told me that "respectable black women don't show off their stomachs either." Why couldn't she just ask me not to wear that shirt because she didn't like it, instead of making it into a race issue?

I felt as though one day couldn't pass without my friends and family mocking something I did that was totally natural for me. They made a race issue out of my looks, my voice, how I pronounced words, and everything I did.

Their remarks always offended me. What did they mean, talking like a white girl? It was ridiculous! I was proud of the education I got at my school. I didn't know how to talk or act in any other way.

It was horrible. The more I strived to speak like an educated person, the more I was considered a white girl by my own race.

I know it doesn't have to be that way. Last summer I visited Spelman College, a historically black women's college in Atlanta, Georgia. The alumni there were extremely smart and had perfect diction.

They were also proud of being black and were sure of their

culture. They showed me that a black person can be and sound educated without losing her black identity. But in my old school, and with my friends and family, that didn't seem to be the case.

Finally, I got fed up and decided to transfer to a different school. I was tired of being examined and analyzed by everyone.

Shortly after I arrived at my new high school, I began to have a whole new outlook on life. I noticed girls of all different sizes had boyfriends, and fine ones, too.

"How did she get him? Look at her size," I would think. Walking the halls, guys commented on girls' butts—but not the way I was used to.

"Look at how round it is, that's so fly," they'd say.

I was really shocked. These guys liked big butts and girls like me? Wow!

I began to forget about my looks and could concentrate on my schoolwork. I knew I had to get my head together, or else. I began to boost up my grades, receive awards, and get asked on trips. I felt really good about myself because I was able to use education as a way to build myself up. Once my marks rose, I felt great.

I thought I knew what guys wanted—white girls, Hispanic girls, or light-skinned black girls with long legs and straight hair.

At the new school, no one commented on the way I talked, acted or dressed. I was kind of expecting them to say something, but they didn't. I'm not sure if I was losing my "white girl" character, or if they just didn't care.

After a while, I began to compare myself to other black females in my life. Many of my black girl friends love themselves, regardless of what size they are.

Where did they get such positive attitudes? My white girl friends from the private school continuously complained about their size and thought they had to be thin to be accepted by men.

It would be great if more white girls had the same positive body image as many black girls. It also would be great if black girls would feel good about showing how educated they are, and would take a lesson from successful black women like the alumni I met at Spelman. Speaking and acting educated doesn't have anything to do with being white or black.

I found out I don't have to look like a white girl or talk like a black girl. It may be best to be right in the middle.

The author was 17 when she wrote this story.

How I Overcame Being Overweight

By Shaniqua Sockwell

Have you ever loved something so much you were willing to go all out for it and not even care about the consequences until later?

Well, I have. I had an addiction that was not only uncomfortable, but unhealthy. It wasn't alcohol or drugs. It was food. And because of my compulsive love of it, I became fat.

Now, I'm not saying there's anything wrong with being chubby, but if you're only 5'1," you shouldn't be gaining weight the way I was at 14. Since I'm so short, all I had was gut, gut, gut. I was not a happy girl.

My problem started around my 13th birthday. The truth of the matter is I love to eat. I've always loved food. Meat (especially sausages), Ben and Jerry's ice cream, cakes and cookies, pizza with extra cheese and pepperoni, Chinese food, and all sorts of take out, from Burger King to Taco Bell. I love it all. Tacos, burritos, fajitas, nachos...you name it, I'll eat it. This became my problem.

I had never been a slender girl—I was always in between. But by the time I turned 13 I was getting too big. Every morning, my father's sausages lured me awake, while late night snacks of cookies and pound cake while watching *The Twilight Zone* were routine. I knew I had to stop, but for some reason, I couldn't.

I'd never been uncomfortable about my weight before because I figured it was hereditary (there are a few overweight people in my family). But suddenly my fears about being overweight came crashing down on me. I began to wonder, "What if I become obese? What if I never stop eating and I never lose some of this weight?"

> **I was afraid that I would get so big that I would wheeze when I bent over, and have problems getting up.**

That year I blew up and started to wear jeans in double sizes, like 12-14. I could barely fit into my pants, causing my next door neighbor's kid to nickname me "Jello Butt." I became so self-conscious I only wore baggy shirts and pants.

My parents knew nothing about how I felt. They assumed, since they gave me all the food I wanted and a roof over my head, I was happy. Wrong. They never brought me aside to discuss the issue. I knew they noticed my growing size (how do you hide this sort of thing?) but I figured either they didn't care to discuss it with me, or they didn't care at all.

I'm not blaming them for my weight problem—that was my fault. To be totally honest, I didn't want to talk about it because I was uncomfortable. I didn't need my parents telling me nonsense or trying to sugar coat the issue by saying, "Oh, that's just baby fat, stop being so self-conscious." Besides, how do you tell your parents you love to eat and then complain that you're getting fat?

Three and a half years went by like this. Finally when I was

16, I looked in the mirror one day and said to myself, "Unh-unh, this ain't happenin'!" I pledged to lose weight before I became obese.

I was as concerned about my health as I was about my looks. Every time I bent over, I felt like I was gonna collapse. I was afraid that I would get so big that I would wheeze or something when I bent over, and that I would have problems getting up, or I would have to walk really slowly because my weight would slow down my pace. I didn't want that to happen.

At the time I had a boyfriend who I was crazy about. At first he didn't seem concerned about my weight. Don't ask me why, but things began to change after a while. He never seemed to want to be seen in public with me, nor would he take me out anywhere. I felt part of what contributed to our break-up was the fact that I thought he was ashamed of my weight, but didn't want to hurt my feelings by telling me.

I finally went on a diet to lose some weight. (I hate exercising.) For the rest of the year, I drank nothing but water, diet soda, and fruit juice. I had a few desserts, but mostly just peppermints. Fast food and my beloved hero sandwiches were out of the question. I put my love of Italian and Mexican food on hold, as well as my dad's sausages and lasagna. I ate more salads and yogurt and vegetables than ever. It was hard to resist temptation—sometimes I can't believe that I did it so well. I will admit that I snuck food from home or ate outside. But basically all my willpower came from me not wanting to ruin my health.

After a few months, I finally lost most of the weight (about 20 lbs). There was only one problem: because I didn't balance my diet, I got a little too skinny. I didn't really notice this until my mother told me.

One day she took my little sister and me out to McDonald's. I ordered only a salad. She turned around and said, "Why don't you get a burger or something and stop this diet nonsense! You're starting to look like a crackhead!" (Mother knows best.)

Through Thick and Thin

I was appalled. I said, "I'm supposed to be your kid and you're calling me a crackhead!" This was the first time she expressed any reaction to my diet at all.

But when I looked in the mirror that night, I saw that my face was completely sunken in. My eyes were hollow. Even though my mother was wrong to come out of her face the way she did, I had to admit that she was right. In a way it was a surprise, being this was the first time she said anything about it. I guess she really did care.

So I balanced my diet and began eating more of what was right for me, like fruits, vegetables, and lots of water. I got plenty of exercise by walking and running to the store for my family.

Now, at age 18, I've finally found a size I'm happy with. Gone are the days of wearing only baggy shirts—I wear tight tops like crazy. I'm finally comfortable with myself and no longer feel ashamed of my body.

"Why don't you get a burger and stop this diet nonsense! You're starting to look like a crackhead!" my mom said.

Of course, there are people who look down on me now that I'm no longer chubby. My mother is one of them. If I come out in a nice outfit, she'll say something like, "You look nice, but you're too skinny. You looked better big." (What a confidence booster!) But other people make me feel real good when they tell me how nice I look and they can't believe it's me. And there are people who didn't know me a couple years ago who can't believe that I was ever heavy to begin with.

That's when I break out my "plump pictures." I'm glad they don't remember me that way, because I didn't want to leave that impression of the old me on the world. I think people like the new me just fine.

Shaniqua was 18 when she wrote this story.

Are Teens Getting Too Fat?

By Megan Cohen

Obesity is a serious issue that isn't just about appearance, but about health. And it's a growing problem in the U.S.

Obesity can worsen asthma, and can cause diabetes, heart problems, and more. It's now the second most common preventable cause of death in the U.S., after smoking.

About 14% of adolescents and children are overweight in the U.S., triple the amount since the 1960s. One problem is the way teens live today. More adolescents are leading a sedentary lifestyle—too much TV and not enough exercise.

Unhealthy food, such as fast food, is aggressively marketed to teens nowadays. Teens consume foods and drinks that have a lot of calories, as well as fat and sugar in them.

To find out more about what causes obesity, and how it can endanger health, I spoke to Dr. Alison Hoppin, Associate

Director for Pediatric Programs at the Massachusetts General Hospital Weight Center.

Q: What is obesity?

A: Obesity is defined as an unhealthy amount of body weight. It's not about appearance, but whether your amount of body weight is leading to medical problems or not. Overweight is defined as a lower degree of that.

Q: What contributes to adolescent obesity?

A: Many things. Some people are born with a natural tendency to gain weight easily. They might have to work extra hard to keep a healthy weight. But what's made obesity more of a problem over the last 30 years has to do with fitness and diet.

Q: What are the health effects of obesity in teens?

A: There are more than 40 different medical problems that are more likely to happen or are more severe if you're obese. Many of those occur in adulthood, but we're seeing more of them in teenagers as well.

For example, a surprising number of teens are getting weight-related diabetes. Obesity can also make asthma worse or cause acid reflux or sleep disorders. And people can have problems with depression. People who feel depressed are more likely to gain weight, and on the flip side, being overweight sometimes leads to depression.

Q: Do some ethnic groups tend to be more obese than others?

A: There are different obesity rates in different ethnic groups. Certain groups may have "easy-gaining" genes—genes that make people more likely to gain weight. Also, different groups may have different access to healthy foods. This can be an economic thing, a cultural thing, or simply about what's available in your neighborhood.

Q: Can somebody who's obese in childhood really change?

A: Yes. Working on your weight in sensible ways when you're younger may even be more effective than working on it in adulthood. It's harder to have a permanent weight change once you've reached adulthood.

Q: How does a teen with a hectic lifestyle start up a new eating regimen?

A: Thinking about what will fit into your lifestyle is the first step. Then figure out what you can commit to permanently. I'd much rather see people make small but permanent changes than go on a crash diet.

Crash diets almost never work in the long run. People may lose a little weight, but they're likely to regain it. Skipping meals isn't a good way of dieting, either. It's not effective and tends to lead to a "fast and binge pattern."

"There are more than 40 different medical problems that are more likely to happen if you're obese," says Dr. Hoppin.

Finding ways of getting exercise into your life is an important piece of the whole picture, too. Teens of all shapes and sizes should find an activity that gets them moving and stick with it. It doesn't matter so much what you do, as long as you do something.

Q: If there's nobody at home to cook your meals, what are some alternatives for healthy eating?

A: A lot of prepared food isn't terribly healthy. So learning to prepare some healthy meals yourself is one approach.

You can also find prepared or packaged meals that are reasonably healthy, but you have to be a smart shopper. Some packaged frozen meals come with accurate nutritional information and reasonable portion size.

But it's important for people to learn how to prepare some

foods, hopefully in a quick and easy way that's also healthy.

Finding vegetables you like (frozen are fine) and making them part of any meal is a great place to start. You can always microwave vegetables, and they'll fill you up without providing a lot of extra calories.

Q: Is it bad to eat while watching TV?

A: Yes. There are three problems with it. One is that you're not getting any activity at all while you're watching TV. Second, many people who eat while watching TV eat out of habit rather than hunger. So you're more likely to eat more than your body needs.

Third, TV has a whole lot of food advertising. It often encourages you to try foods that might not be healthy and to eat when you're not hungry.

And for younger kids, some of the advertising also implies that kids don't like healthy food—that kid food is chicken fingers and French fries. If you get into those habits when you're young, it's hard to broaden your horizons.

Q: How about what we drink—does that contribute to our weight?

A: Yes. The calories that people drink are kind of hidden. Kids get a lot more calories than they think from drinking juice, regular soda, or sports drinks. Even if it's 100% juice or a sports drink, it's basically sugar. And if someone has six or seven servings of these drinks every day, that's as many calories as a Big Mac.

Megan was 16 when she conducted this interview.

The War of the Weights

By Elizabeth Thompson

Everywhere you go, there is a battle between slim girls and thick girls.

The weapons are looks or words like: "Now, she knows she can't fit into those jeans. I don't even know why she wore them. The zipper can't zip that size 12 waist when it's a size 5 pants. What she needs to do is take her fat butt home 'cause she ain't cute."

Or: "Now look at this bony girl wearing that skirt, she looks like she's about to break. Does the child ever eat? I know she don't think she's cute with those chicken legs."

Words like these sound familiar? Of course they do, because we've all heard them (maybe a little less severely) from friends, family and jealous people. Sometimes they even come straight out of our own mouths.

Your appearance is the first thing people see when they look at you, and if they don't like what they see, they will criticize you and sometimes even hate you without knowing you.

People are always talking about other people's figures. You see it all the time on talk shows, where there's a 300-lb lady in a leopard-print mini skirt saying she looks better than the skinny girl on the panel because she has more to strut.

And at family reunions there's that one aunt who has about eight kids and has never gained a pound who brags about how you're gonna wish you look like her when you get that old.

To tell you the truth, girls fight in these battles more than boys do. It seems like girls are always making bad comments about other girls' figures when they know those comments would hurt them if the tables were turned.

When someone says something negative about your body, it affects how you feel about everything else.

I'm 16 years old, am 5'7," and weigh 112 lbs. People are always commenting on my body. I always used to pay more attention to the negative comments than the positive. I thought there was something really wrong with me, and I hated my figure.

They said things like: "You're too skinny, you need to eat more." And, "You're too skinny to be showing your legs."

My body was always on my mind. I felt like the whole world was looking at me and couldn't wait to say something. I felt people were telling me the truth, and it was my job to do something about it.

Even though I got mad and told them I didn't care, I would go home and look in the mirror to see what was wrong. I knew I was skinny, but I just didn't know what was so bad about it. I worried too much about what other people thought, and if they didn't like what they saw, I surely didn't want to be it.

Eventually, though, I realized that there is nothing wrong with me and stopped paying attention to everyone's stupid comments. Now I look in the mirror and love it because I don't see who I want to be or what the world wants me to be. I just see myself.

But for many girls, it's not that easy to get over feeling bad about their bodies. Some girls starve themselves, dress in baggy clothes, or don't want to party or go out, all because of what other people think.

It doesn't help that girls are constantly being told what's wrong with them. If girls were told what's good about them, they might not worry so much.

The worst part is that we often hear those nasty comments right at home. It seems like family members feel it's their job to tell you that you're too fat, too skinny, too tall, too loud.

Besides teaching you manners and morals, your family helps you figure out your identity. So why should parents and family members make it harder for you by telling you that you're too fat or too skinny? I think it's terrible that little kids have to hear nasty comments right at home.

My 4-year-old niece already gets comments about being overweight. She just says what older girls say—that she's not fat, she's big-boned. She even says she's on a diet, while asking for a second plate of macaroni and cheese with an innocent and adorable smile on her face.

For now, she doesn't really mind the remarks because she's still in her world of innocence and toys. But later on, I hope she doesn't hold on to her hurt.

I love my niece's size, and I can't imagine her any other way. Maybe that's how she's supposed to be. Maybe everyone is supposed to be the way they are, and that's why changing our bodies is so hard.

To tell you the truth, there's nothing wrong with being thick or slim. So girls shouldn't make rude comments about each other's bodies. Our bodies show our uniqueness, style, identity and femininity. And when someone says something negative about your body, it affects how you feel about everything else, too.

Your weight doesn't affect your education, talents or goals, but your self-esteem does. When that's low, your whole life can seem low when it's truly not.

Girls should boost up each other's self-esteem, no matter what size they are. Even if you don't like the way someone looks, that's not a reason to hate her or think you're better than her.

I think if a girl is respectable, has a nice personality, or is doing something positive, that's the number one thing she should be complimented on. People should comment on a girl's personality, not on her size.

Elizabeth was 17 when she wrote this story. She went on to college and earned a degree in journalism.

Naturally Thin

By Desirée Guéry

When I walk into a room, it feels like everyone looks at me. No, I'm not a super model. I'm just a normal teenage Latina with brown eyes and straight brown hair. I usually wear comfortable clothing, like blue jeans and T-shirts. Nothing fancy, nothing racy.

But at 5'6" and 105 lbs, I am thinner than the "average" girl, wearing size small shirts and size 3 jeans and skirts. I was called a "stick figure" in elementary school because of my thin arms and legs.

And now, years later, I can't count the times that people have gasped when they saw me, and then whispered to the person beside them, "She's so skinny!"

Those are the polite ones. Some people feel the need to shout it out. After I turned 14, I started to get the infamously rude "cat calls" from guys on the street, who said things like, "You're skinny, but that's OK! Sexy anyway."

And I had to deal with one particularly humiliating moment last winter, as a new student in my high school. As soon as I walked into my English class, two girls I didn't know—I'll call them Laura and Mary—ceased their conversation to stare at me.

"Oh my God!" Laura said, causing everyone to stare in our direction. "You are so skinny! I mean, look at you! You're skin and bones!"

It felt like she was being so loud that even people in another state could hear her. I couldn't tell if she meant it as a compliment or an insult.

"That's mean," Mary told her.

I knew other classmates were staring, so I took my seat in front of them and sat down quietly, mustering up a smile, not saying anything. I thought maybe if I ignored her, she'd shut up.

I often stare at myself in the mirror, trying to find what's so weird about me. What would make me acceptable?

"It's not mean. It's the truth!" said Laura. "Come on now. Have you even eaten this year?" She continued on and on until I turned around and said, "Just because I'm 20 lbs skinnier than you doesn't mean you have the right to announce it to the world. There are plenty of things I could say about your weight."

"Oooh," said our fellow classmates. After a moment of silence, Laura said, "God, you don't have to be so rude about it." She was the one being rude, but I just left it at that.

People's comments have made me feel self-conscious about my weight. Because it's fashionable to be thin, I know that some people point out my weight as a compliment, which feels good to hear. But when people make a big deal about how skinny I am, it makes me feel like an object. Each time they stare, I feel low, like an outcast.

I hadn't noticed that I was thinner than most others until I went to elementary school, where I realized I was the skinniest one in my class. My kindergarten teacher even gave me extra snacks. I didn't know it was an attempt to fatten me up. I just assumed I was special.

My grandmother and mother used to give me food all the time as well. I ate and ate and ate, asked for more because I was still hungry, ate some more, but always stayed the same weight. I have a high metabolism, which means I burn calories quickly. So to this day, no matter how much I eat, I don't gain weight.

Being thin isn't that common in my family. The only two relatives I know who're skinny are my uncle Eddie and my grandmother. Everyone else is either "normal" or slightly chubby, which makes me stand out.

So family members usually try to fatten me up at holiday dinners. Even though they know I'm naturally thin, it doesn't stop them from hitting me with a round of questions if I don't finish my plate.

"Do you feel sick?" "Are you full already?" "Do you want something else to eat?" I prefer to suck it up and eat rather than be interrogated for not eating.

To make matters worse, some people who don't know me well wonder if I'm bulimic or anorexic. I've had doctors ask me about my eating habits, fearful that I was starving myself. Friends joke about me having an eating disorder (although I don't laugh), and strangers insinuate it with their looks of pity.

It hurts, because I can't believe people could automatically assume that about me. Why can't I be naturally thin without starving myself? I can't change, and I wish people didn't make me feel like I have to.

I often go home and stare at myself in the mirror, trying to find what's so weird about me. I don't see myself as being extremely skinny, but after all the stares and random comments from people on the street, I question myself as I stare. "What would make me acceptable? Should I wear baggy clothes so that

I look bigger?" I wonder.

At times, I wear baggier outfits that make me look like I weigh more, even though loose clothes make me feel uncomfortable because they feel as if they're going to fall off.

Sometimes I ask myself, "If I were prettier, would people still gawk at me? If they did, would they mean it in a nicer way?" So I try to make myself more attractive by wearing more makeup or trendier clothes.

But, at other times, I don't care what anyone thinks of my weight. I hear the same comments so often that they sometimes bounce off me as if I'm immune to them.

> **When people make a big deal about how skinny I am, it makes me feel like an object.**

I still usually wear fitted clothes, because it makes me feel like myself. And I try to focus on the positive comments from my family and friends. Some of my friends tell me I'm so lucky to be as thin as I am, especially because I can eat as much as I do without gaining weight.

If I'm out to eat with my friends and I order dessert, they'll say something like, "Oh, I can't order anything. I'm too fat for that."

But they're not fat, they're just not as thin as me. Either way, they're perfect the way they are. It's silly that they won't eat a slice of cake or an ice cream cone once in a while. I feel lucky that I can enjoy eating whatever I want.

Plus, I can always squeeze into seats when there's hardly any room. If I drop something in a small space, I can always get it. There are plenty of great things about being thin.

But as I struggle to become comfortable with my weight, someone's comments always get me down again. I went to the pizzeria for lunch a few days ago to get a slice of baked ziti pizza. As the man behind the counter got my slice, he looked back and forth from the slice to me.

"You sure you can eat this? Maybe you should get a plain

slice," he said. "It's smaller."

"Why wouldn't I be able to eat it?" I asked, trying not to get upset.

"Well, you're a small girl. You might not eat it all."

"I know what I want," I replied. "And if you don't want to serve it to me, I can go elsewhere."

With that note, he put the slice in the oven. Incidents like this make me wonder if I'll ever be completely comfortable with my weight. But they won't stop me from trying.

Desirée was 16 when she wrote this story.

Overboard With Exercise

By Shavone Harris

Got to make it home, got to make it home. I only got 40 minutes and there's 40 or 50 more blocks to go. Puff, puff, pant, wheeze! I've got to pedal faster. My legs are burning and I can feel the dryness in my throat.

"Beep-beeeeep!" Without a bell on my bike, I have to make my own noise to get the pedestrians to move out of my way. "Excuse me, watch out!" I scream as a girl comes out of the hair salon.

Bang! I hit the girl.

My bike stops, but I keep going, banging my head on the pavement, scraping my elbow, bruising my knee and rolling into a parking meter. (Now I see why parents nag us about helmets.)

I lie there wondering, "Why, why, why? Why can't I just take a chill pill? Why do I go overboard when it comes to sports and exercise?"

Maybe I shouldn't have ridden my bike so far, but I was trying to work off the calories of the Italian ice I ate. There's nothing like exercise for keeping in shape.

Even though the girl and I were OK, my recent bike accident has made me think about my life-long affair with sports and exercise. When I was younger, I was overweight and not very popular. Playing sports was the only time when I could fit in with the other kids. It made me feel good about myself and helped me build my will power and determination.

But the acceptance I got from being good at sports was so important to me that sometimes I would get carried away. Even now, my determination to do well sometimes makes me a danger to myself. I push myself so hard that it hurts.

It all started back in elementary school. The other kids wouldn't play with me and I was never picked for any team.

The only time I felt popular was when it was time to choose teams.

One day during recess, my 2nd grade teacher made the kids choose me for a game of kickball. Little did I (or anyone else) know that I could kick harder and farther than anyone else on the playground.

I remember how good it felt when my foot hit the ball, or when I made the winning point. After that day at recess, I was always chosen or fought over—on the playground, anyway. The only time I felt popular was when it was time to choose teams.

My surprise success at kickball made me want to try other sports and activities. I learned them quickly and even excelled at some of them. I also had my share of mishaps, but they just motivated me to push myself harder.

One day, full of kickball-inspired confidence, I thought I'd show the older kids that I could ride a bike as fast as they could.

I took the bike to the top of a hill, got on it and pushed down, but my shoelaces got caught in the bike chain. The bike fell over and I went sliding down the hill. I felt like an idiot after everyone, including an old woman, laughed at me.

Not only was I bruised, I was hurt emotionally, because everyone was laughing at me. The bike chain was popped, so I couldn't get back on and try again.

I had to walk home as a failure and disappointment to myself. I never wanted to feel like that again. So I decided to try harder; next time I would not give up.

Jumping rope restored my athletic glory. In 3rd grade, I became a speed jumper. I was proud that I could jump rope really fast. But I learned the hard way that if you go too fast and you suddenly mess up, your ankles and legs will get whipped.

Later, in 4th, 5th, and 6th grades, I taught myself how to Rollerblade and skateboard.

One summer I spent a month at my cousin's house. I hung around with him and his male friends because I had no one else to play with. They used to Rollerblade and skateboard down the slides at the neighborhood park. They dared me to jump off the slide on skates and the skateboard. I was terrified, but they said that since I was a girl (a big, hefty girl), I couldn't do it.

If I followed my common sense, I would take a break when I'm feeling pain. But I don't stop.

Their comments killed my fear; I had to prove them wrong. That day I learned the meaning of the expression "the bigger they are, the harder they fall." The two back wheels on the skateboard got hooked on the edge of the slide and I fell flat on my face. I was in a lot of pain. I had a busted lip and a busted ego.

To patch up my ego, I decided to try it again, but this time on Rollerblades. But when I tried it with the blades, I jumped too early and once again slid off the slide on my face and arms.

I was in so much pain I could feel my body throbbing. No one tried to help me. I wanted to cry, but I didn't want to seem weak. They were all laughing at me. So I got up as angry as ever and tried it again.

The looks on their faces were to die for as I jumped up and made my first 360 degree turn, and landed as best as I could backwards. I felt even better when none of them could do a full 360 in the air.

From 7th through 10th grade, I was hooked on volleyball, softball, basketball, and tennis. Unfortunately, though, the girls I played with didn't care about winning anymore. And they were so concerned about their long nails, they couldn't hit properly. I was hit by so many balls, I can still see the dents and Spaulding logos on my forehead. But the guys respected my abilities and that felt good.

The summer before junior year I lost a lot of weight. When I came back to school in the fall, it was as if nobody knew the old me. I felt more popular; everybody talked to me. It felt great. But I still wanted to tone up, so I took body-building for gym.

Although I was new to weight training, I wanted to be the best at it. When the class began, I was lifting 30 lbs with my arms, legs, and back. Every week I would increase the weight by 10 lbs. At the end of the class, five months later, I was lifting five times more weight than when I had started.

As I progressed, I noticed the boys watching me. They began to include me in their weight-lifting club (an in-class group of hardcore students), and they gave me more respect than they gave the other girls in the class.

We began friendly competitions. They called me "Black Xena" and "Black Chyna" (after the professional wrestler) and I had a lot of them as friends and trainers. I wanted to be strong like Chyna, so I liked my nicknames. If the big, strong guys were respecting me, I knew I must be good. It motivated me to continue working out.

I liked that weight training gave me muscles and improved my figure. But I sometimes got Charley horses and cramps in my legs, and pains in my arms and shoulders from lifting so much weight.

Then about a month ago when I went with my sister to her gym, I put 100 lbs on the machine to work my upper inner thighs and I pulled my muscles. It hurt a little, but I continued working out. That made it worse, until, days later, I woke up and I couldn't move my legs.

You'd think I'd learn, but the dumb part is that I didn't let it stop me. No pain, no gain, I said to myself.

I know I tend to go overboard with physical activities. Part of that is because it feels so great to do well at something that an average heavy person wouldn't be good at. Being one of the best at sports also earned me the respect and acceptance that I didn't get from my peers before.

I realize now that my determination to gain acceptance from my peers, and to succeed in sports and exercise, seems to have killed my common sense. My common sense tells me to stop when I feel pain, but I don't.

I keep going. If I followed my common sense, I would take a break when I'm feeling pain or feeling lightheaded. But I don't stop because then I feel lazy and I worry I'm going to gain back my old weight. I want to feel like I'm always pumping myself up.

I admit that part of my obsession with exercise, especially now, is due to my desire to lose weight. Being slimmer makes me feel more accepted, which is why it's hard to cut back on my exercising.

But now that I'm close to my goal, I know I need to slow down. I'm trying to channel my passion for working out into soft-core exercises like jogging and power walking.

I still love to "feel the burn," but I know I need to chill. I had a nightmare recently in which I hurt myself so badly I looked like a pretzel. I don't want that to happen in real life.

Shavone was 17 when she wrote this story.

I Took Dieting Too Far

By Renu George

When I was really little, I was thin and I could tell that was a good thing to be. I was praised for my picky eating habits, while my chubby cousin was reprimanded for putting an extra helping of rice on her plate. My parents used up rolls of film just on me. I would always pose and smile a toothy grin, which led my relatives to predict a future career in modeling for me.

I was 7 years old when I began to gain weight. I spent the summer in India with my grandmother, who wouldn't stop feeding me Indian sweets and curries. I came back to America with a sweet tooth and a lot of clothes that no longer fit me.

My parents chided me softly, saying that I was beginning to look like my fat cousin. I began sneaking cups of ice cream from the kitchen to my bedroom, so that I wouldn't have to see the disappointment in their eyes when I ate. The boasts about my finicky eating stopped. My father started calling me "rolly-poly" and wouldn't let me wear shorts outside in the company of his friends.

By the time I was 8, I was totally self-conscious about my weight. One day, while my 3rd grade teacher was reading to us, I stared at the sight of my thighs spread out over my chair. They seemed so huge to me, oozing out in every direction. While the other kids sat at the edge of their seats, wondering what would happen next, I was drawing pictures in my mind of how fat I must look in my little yellow sweatpants—like a tub of butter.

In 5th grade, I learned that the old children's rhyme, "Sticks and stones may break my bones, but words will never hurt me," was one of the biggest lies ever spoken. Whenever we had a fight, my friends would make mooing sounds, or pretend the floor was shaking when I walked by. We would always hug and make up the next day, but part of me felt that if I weren't fat, no one would make fun of me anymore.

Losing weight became like a game. I wanted to see how many pounds I could lose and how fast.

Things got worse when I entered middle school. I started to read the teen magazines that told you how girls were supposed to look. My thoughts also began to turn from hopscotch and jump rope to guys. I noticed that they smiled more appreciatively at the skinny little girls than at me. Whenever I passed by mirrors, windows, or any shiny object that showed my reflection, I'd stare sadly at the chubby girl looking back at me.

I started looking for "Get thin quick" diets. I planned the great wardrobes that I would buy when I lost weight. But I never seemed to make it past Day 3 of the 30-day plans. I never stuck to them because they could never accomplish what I wanted: to wake up one morning, thin and happy.

Toward the end of 8th grade, I decided to do something besides fantasize about how I wanted to look. A friend, who was also overweight, and I decided that we would go away for the summer and come back to 9th grade very thin. When school let out, I left for camp.

When I got there and saw the food, I didn't think that I would be able to keep up my end of the bargain. Even though there were four lunch lines serving different foods, everything was either fried and soaked in oil, or fried and soaked in oil with cheese on top. And at the end of every line, they had what was basically an ice cream store. There were so many different flavors and cones that it seemed almost sinful to let it go to waste.

After about a week, I signed up for a step aerobics class. It was either that, ballroom dancing with a bunch of pubescent, acne-covered boys, or sitting in the weight room all day, waiting for the macho guys to finish hogging the equipment. I started doing aerobics for an hour every day.

At the end of the day, I would add up all of the calories that I had burned by exercising. That made me feel so good that I decided to try skipping the ice cream at lunch. After I did, I felt so proud of myself that the next day I wanted to go even further. I decided to skip the ice cream at dinner, too.

It became like a dare for me. How far could I go before I cracked? Could I stand the pressure? I ate a little bit less each day. At the end of two weeks, I had lost 6 lbs. It wasn't that much but I already felt as if all my clothes were loose on me. I felt prettier and thinner.

After getting home from camp, I continued my dieting. Losing weight became like a game. I wanted to see how many pounds I could lose and how fast. When my body craved ice cream, I would try to ignore the sensation and force Jello down my throat instead. I tried to fill up my day with activities so that I wouldn't have time to think about food. At the end of the day, I would count up the calories I had consumed and feel proud that I had been able to resist temptation. It was this feeling that kept me going.

When I started high school that fall, I began playing volleyball. Since I was exercising vigorously, I continued to lose weight steadily. By the end of the season, I had lost 17 lbs and reached my ideal weight. At least that was my doctor's opinion. But I still wasn't satisfied.

I wanted to keep losing weight but, after volleyball season ended, the pounds no longer rolled off quite so effortlessly. I worried that I would become fat again. At the same time, I began to miss candy bars and ice cream pops. It had been almost five months since I had eaten a piece of chocolate and carrots had lost their appeal as a snack food. That's when I discovered the wonderful world of fat-free eating. Candy, cookies, and even some types of ice cream were available in fat-free varieties. For a while, I became a fat-free addict.

Unfortunately, fat-free food tastes like crap, so eventually I stopped eating it. I began to think of other ways to cut down my fat consumption, such as becoming a vegetarian and skipping meals. If I ate three full meals a day, I felt bad about myself.

Losing 7 lbs in one week wasn't normal, it was frightening.

In the spring, I joined the track team because I thought that I needed to lose more weight for shorts season. I would run between three and five miles a day. But the more weight I lost, the more unhappy I was with the way I looked. I was too thin in some places and too fat in others. I would spend hours in front of the mirror looking at each part of my body, finding flaws. Every time I passed a window or shiny object, I checked my reflection to see if my thighs had gotten any bigger since morning.

I started feeling guilty about everything I ate. My parents would take me out for pizza. After just one slice (that I had blotted all the oil off) I would feel fat. I saw every piece of food, no matter how low in calories, as something that would cause me to gain weight. After eating, I would touch my stomach to see if it had gotten any bigger; I felt like the food was gathering up in little folds across my waist.

One night, I had to make peanut butter cookies for a school bake sale. I tasted part of one cookie in each batch to see if they were cooked or not. It was such a small amount of cookie, but afterwards I began to have that familiar feeling of fat growing in my body. It was 10 p.m., but I began doing crunches. I did more than 200 crunches that night. Doing the crunches themselves wasn't the bad part, it was the fact that I felt that eating even one cookie was a sin. I thought that I had broken a promise to myself to be thin.

The original idea of pushing myself to the limit was still present in my mind. I wanted to see how far I could go before I had to stop. I wanted to see what it would take for my willpower to crack, for my brain to cry, "Enough!"

One day I had an English muffin with nothing on it and a glass of water for breakfast, and fat-free cereal with skim milk and an apple for lunch. After school, I ran three miles on less than 300 calories. Considering all the calories I burned by running, I was in bad shape afterwards. I felt very dizzy. All the blood rushed to my head, and I thought that I was going to black out. But I still didn't feel like I had gone too far.

When I jokingly told a friend about the incident, he gave me a funny look and said, "That's not a good idea. Don't ever do it again." He wasn't the only one who thought I was overdoing it. A lot of my friends were getting tired of the fact that I wouldn't eat at McDonald's and that I made comments about the fat content in the food they ate. My parents had begun to complain that I was becoming too skinny and that my bones were sticking out. Then one day my best friend said to me, "You really are beginning to look anorexic."

Not long after that there was a week when I lost a pound a day. Suddenly, my parents' comments about my becoming unhealthy started echoing in my head. Losing 7 lbs in one week wasn't normal, it was frightening. It was the kind of thing that happened in TV movies about anorexia. I was afraid to get back on the scale because I didn't want to find out that I had lost another pound.

For the first time in a year, I looked in the mirror and really saw myself. My wrists had become scrawny and I was losing my hips. This wasn't the image that I had in mind when I started out. I had wanted to look slim and in shape, but instead I looked emaciated and bony. I had thought my friends were out of line when they said that I was worrying too much about what I ate. Now, I realized that they had been right.

Denying myself the food I wanted had become such a big part of my life that I couldn't imagine getting through the day without it. If I was going to get over that, I had to stop believing that every piece of food I put in my mouth would automatically make me fat. I had to recognize that since I was much more physically active now than when I was young and chubby, I didn't have to starve myself to stay in shape. I had to realize that what I was becoming was not attractive. Being overly skinny was just as bad as being overweight. And the people around me had begun to get annoyed and even repulsed by the way I was so concerned about my appearance.

I will always be glad that I was able to lose weight, and I think that initially I had the right idea. I started by eating less junk food and exercising more, both of which are healthy things to do. But then I let myself get caught up in the fantasy of becoming some sort of supermodel. I became so obsessed with losing weight that I lost touch with reality. To get over that, I had to start listening to the people around me. I had to hear them when they told me that it was OK to eat a full meal. I had to start believing them when they said I wasn't fat.

I wish I could say that I was completely cured. I wish I could say that I have stopped checking nutrition labels and counting calories. But happily ever after doesn't come so easy. There are still days when guilt washes over me after I eat a full meal. I have to stop and remind myself that it's OK. But each day the guilt becomes smaller and easier to deal with.

And then there are the good days, when I don't think about my weight at all.

Renu was 16 when she wrote this story.

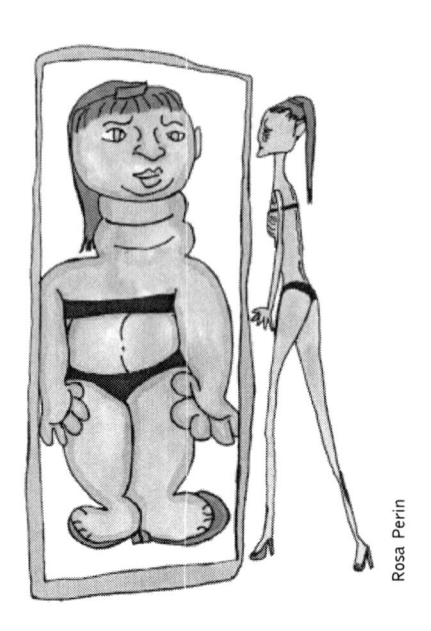

What Are Eating Disorders?

By Stephanie Perez

Dr. Katie Gentile is the director of the Women's Center at John Jay College in New York City and has a PhD in counseling psychology. I interviewed her to find out more about eating disorders.

Q: What is anorexia?

A: Anorexia is an eating disorder in which you quit eating, or eat only minimal amounts of food. People can end up losing 20% of their body weight. If you're a woman, you typically lose your period.

Q: What is bulimia?

A: Bulimia is an eating disorder in which usually someone eats a lot of food in a short period of time, a lot more than most people. That's called binging. Then they make up for it. They might throw it up, take diet pills, or take laxatives. That's called a purge. Maybe they don't eat for a long period of time or they exercise a lot.

Some people have both anorexia and bulimia. You can binge and purge when you're anorexic. You can be anorexic if you binge and purge.

There's also a binge-eating disorder, which is bulimia without the purging. You binge but you don't throw up.

Q: Who develops eating disorders?

A: The stereotype is that anorexia affects only rich white girls, but that's not true. And binge eating and bulimia in particular happen in more diverse populations. People in all cultures may develop it.

Eating disorders happen mostly to women, but about 10% of anorexics are men. Up to 30% of bulimics might be men.

Q: What problems can these disorders cause?

A: Anorexia is a form of starvation. You can lose your hair, your skin starts peeling, you grow body hair—like fur—you're cold all over all the time. And even if you begin to gain weight after being anorexic, you can still have problems. It can affect your hormones, your thyroid, your heart.

With bulimia, it depends on how you're purging. If you're throwing up, you can burn away your esophagus with stomach acid. Your teeth can begin to decay. You can develop stomach and digestive problems. If you take laxatives, you can get hemorrhoids and you can destroy your intestines.

This is really dangerous. It's not just a diet.

Stephanie was 17 when she conducted this interview.

For information on how to overcome an eating disorder, see "Recovering From an Eating Disorder" on p. 105.

Stephanie Wilson

Starving for Acceptance

By Anonymous

In 6th grade, I was a chubby 10-year-old. In 7th grade, I still had what was considered "baby fat" while every other girl was blooming into her pre-teens, or at least it seemed that way to me.

Being a bit chubby usually didn't bother me. But sometimes the popular boys would say I was a fat pig who no man would ever love, and that I'd grow up to be a lonely old woman staring out the window of my apartment. I wasn't the only victim of their teasing, but since I wasn't popular I felt alone and ugly.

I envied the girls who wore the tight pants and tank tops that showed their belly a little. My mom wouldn't let me dress that way. Instead, I wore long-sleeved shirts with baggy pants. It's not that I wanted to wear those sexier, more revealing clothes. But I felt like all the girls in my school were perfect, beautiful swimsuit models and I was the fat ugly duckling.

The junior high prom was approaching. I saw it as the time to look grown up and beautiful. I didn't want to be the girl standing alone in the corner with everyone dancing around me.

I was tired of people teasing me, so I decided to lose weight by dieting. Around October of 8th grade, I started to eat only crackers and tuna fish with salad dressing for lunch.

I soon grew tired of eating tuna every day. Before, I'd had sandwiches or hot soup for lunch. So I started to have a handful of crackers with cheese instead.

Then I got tired of that, too, and I stopped eating everything but crackers. I felt like I couldn't eat anything else for lunch or I'd never lose the weight I wanted to.

I'd never cared for breakfast because I find it too heavy a meal too early in the day. So I didn't eat breakfast. Dinner was just a small bowl of rice and some beans. I ate dinner with my mom, who usually cooked rice, beans, and some kind of meat, like pork chops or steak. She knew that I wasn't a big fan of meat so she didn't pay attention to the fact that I skipped over it and also ate less rice and beans.

I felt hungry the first weeks of my diet, and my stomach hurt a lot. I was also experiencing headaches and dizziness, and I was tired all the time. I kept wanting to eat something to make the pain go away, but I was afraid to eat and then feel too full. Feeling full made me feel fat.

After some time, I got used to the way I was feeling and began eating even less. I ate crackers every other day for lunch for four months. On the days that I didn't eat crackers, I didn't eat anything at all.

I started to lose weight, and I felt good about myself. I was getting thinner, and I knew that it wouldn't be long before all the baby fat would be gone.

While Mom didn't notice my smaller portions, she noticed I was losing weight. She just thought it was a sign of puberty and growing up. She'd comment on how I was looking slimmer because I was getting taller, and becoming a "young lady."

Through Thick and Thin

I was pleased with my diet plan until one day, halfway through the year, a friend asked if I thought one of our classmates, who'd lost weight recently, was anorexic. I didn't know what the word anorexic meant, so she told me it was a person who didn't eat, just to lose weight. She also told me that anorexia is a psychological disease that kills.

That's when I realized that I might have a problem. I'd made myself think I was an overweight cow who needed to dramatically lose weight, that if I could only lose the weight, I'd be perfect. All of a sudden I felt like I was committing a terrible sin, like I was a witness to a horrific crime but hiding out instead of testifying in court.

I ate crackers for lunch, and the days that I didn't eat crackers, I didn't eat anything at all.

I became disgusted when I realized that I was losing the weight through self-starvation. But I liked losing the weight, and I still had my goal to reach: the prom.

From September 2000 to June 2001, I went from 125 lbs to 99 lbs. During the process of losing weight, I felt proud because I felt like I finally had control over my body fat.

I knew I looked stunning in my prom dress. But I felt like crap—physically and emotionally. I knew how I'd lost my weight. I was starving myself. I thought I was in control but I was wrong. It was unhealthy, and I knew it.

I was aware of how beautiful I looked, but I still wasn't happy with myself. I felt empty because I knew I'd never be satisfied with my appearance. I felt worthless because even after I lost the weight, people in my school still treated me like crap. Now instead of calling me "cow" or "pig," they called me "monkey." And I felt sick because I was always getting headaches and having a feeling of wanting to vomit.

I wanted to stay forever thin at 99 lbs, so when I got to high school, I continued skipping breakfast and would go to the library instead of lunch. But toward the middle of the year, I found I couldn't concentrate during 40-minute classes. I was stressed out and realized that I had to start eating something, anything, during the day to keep me energized.

So I started eating breakfast every morning—a bagel with cream cheese and chocolate milk. I would've eaten something lighter, but they don't sell light meals in my school, and I didn't have healthy food at home.

Every morning I had this breakfast and at home I ate a regular-size plate of food with rice, meat and beans. At the end of freshman year, I weighed 110 lbs. I liked that weight. I was only a bit heavier than I'd been in 8th grade, but I was also healthy.

Sophomore year I stopped eating breakfast again because I wanted to get to school a little later. Instead, I started to eat the school lunch. With meals like pizza, tacos, and chicken nuggets, the weight just piled on me. I was back to 125 lbs by June.

Eventually, my weight got to me again and in January of my junior year, I cut down on my eating habits once more. I stopped buying soda every day, and I stopped eating the rice in school.

At home I'd eat vegetables only or not eat anything at all. In a matter of weeks, my stomach was shrinking, I wasn't feeling hungry anymore, and I knew that I was back on the anorexia track.

When I'd lost about 7 lbs, one of my mom's friends approached me and said, "Oh, my God! You lost so much weight. You look good, though. Keep going—it'll do you good." She made me feel like I'd been a huge balloon before.

When some of my friends told me that I'd lost weight, I felt like they were worried. They'd tell me that I should eat something because I was skinny enough.

I was glad they cared about me, but mostly I felt annoyed when they tried dragging me to Wendy's. I felt that it was my body and they shouldn't tell me what to do with it or force me to eat something I didn't want to eat.

But when people didn't say anything about my weight change, I felt as though I hadn't lost enough for them to notice.

I reached 104 lbs last April. My clothes were huge on me. I liked the way I looked, but I wanted to get back to 99 lbs.

I still long to be super-model thin. Watching the Miss America pageants, the fashion runways, and the music videos with pretty girls in cool outfits, I want to be them. I want to be able to dress in all the latest fashions like the mini-mini skirts and tube tops (not on a daily basis, just dressing up to go out somewhere), without worrying about fat flowing over the rims. I know I could tone my stomach with exercise, but I feel like I don't have time for that.

In the past, no one told me that I was beautiful, pretty, or even attractive. All I ever heard was that I was "cute." Cute—a term I connect with children filled with baby fat.

People still call me "cute," and I hate it. But people do accept me more than in middle school. They don't tease me anymore. Maybe it has something to do with their being more mature, or the fact that I went to a different high school than most of my middle school classmates. But I also feel that it's because now I am what mainstream society wants—the perfect size.

I'm the perfect size, but I'm still not content.

I have more friends and an active social life. I even have a boyfriend, a boyfriend who has told me numerous times that he loves me no matter what. He knows I'm self-conscious about my body, and he helps me by telling me that I'm perfect the way I am. He also tells me, "Love is not about appearances. It's about the beauty within." He makes me feel like I don't have to lose weight to please his eye.

Sometimes it makes me wonder why I do crash diets anyway. If he loves me, then I should love myself and not worry about my weight. I know I'm the perfect size, but I'm still not content. My life isn't perfect—I'm stressed about getting into college, I'm worried about people not liking me, I'm afraid of people finding out what's wrong with me.

I don't have any control over these things, but I do have control over what I eat. I continue to not eat, but it's not an everyday thing. I usually diet, stop dieting, gain weight, get disgusted and do the cycle over and over again.

I know that I have an eating disorder, but every time I try to control it, to eat normally, I hate the way I look and feel, so I go back to my old ways, hoping that the fat will leave my system. I know I'm damaging my body by not eating, but I feel like it's the only way for me to lose weight.

I don't want to have this constant feeling that I'm fat and need to lose weight. People look at me and say, "Damn, I didn't know you were that skinny! You should eat a hamburger!" So I know that to everyone else I am thin.

I do want a way to balance my health and appearance, but it's so hard. Sometimes I get so hungry that I just want to eat and eat and eat until I feel sick and want to throw up. But other times I don't want to even look at food because I know I'd feel sick if I ate it. I know I need to moderate the amount of food I eat but it feels too hard for me.

The pressure that was once from my peers no longer exists. I am the only one who is forcing me to think negatively about my body. I don't want to feel this way, yet I do. I feel as if two people are pulling me in different directions and I'm being torn.

I want to be thin, but I want to be happy with myself. Yes, people have learned to accept me. Now I'm the one who has to learn how to accept myself.

The author was 17 when she wrote this story.

Male on the Scale

By Anonymous

I am a male anorexic. I finally admitted it. If you saw me, you probably wouldn't know. Actually, nobody really suspects it. When I hang out with people and they want something to eat, I just say I'm not that hungry and nibble on some fries.

On average, I eat one meal a day, and maybe a peanut butter and jelly sandwich an hour later. I skip breakfast and I skip lunch. I eat dinner because I have to, though if I can get away with it, I won't. I don't fully understand why I do it. I just do.

Let me stop lying—I know exactly why. It started when I came out of rehab. I was fat because the only thing you do is eat and sleep and sit all day. When I got out I was 187 lbs, about 50 lbs heavier than I'd been only three months before.

I didn't really worry about it until my friends started to tease me. Everybody was like, "Damn, you fat now." People who I used to tease finally had something to get back at me about. A kid who was always chubby would come up to me like, "Damn, what happened to you? You used to be all built and skinny. Now look at your fat ass!" I had to deal with this every day.

To me, being fat was like having a scarlet letter on my chest. I mean, fat people are the ones who get picked on the most. When I was skinny, everybody didn't have jokes, but when I was fat, I got cracked on everywhere.

I started to beat myself up mentally. I'd go shopping for pants and be mad that I couldn't fit in a 34 and still have them baggy. I was mad 'cause my fingers had gotten so fat my ring wouldn't fit. I was a pretty boy before I got fat, but after, I was too afraid to walk around in "wife beaters" and open shirts, 'cause the fat jokes would never end.

I was so ashamed, I let it get to me. I'd look at myself in the mirror and curse at my body. I'd tell myself I was the ugliest and fattest person I'd ever seen. I became hateful of my new weight and decided it had to go.

At first I was eating like I have my whole life: at least two servings of every meal, one if it was nasty. But one night I decided to see if I could make myself throw up after I ate dinner. A friend of mine had confided to me that before I met her she was fat, but she started to throw up her food and that's how she was able to look the way she did.

I thought about what she said and decided to try it myself. It was hard the first time. I thought I was gonna throw up my stomach! But about a week or two after that, I would throw up dinner four times out of the week. Then I started to do the same thing after lunch.

One time, I got caught in the act. I was in the bathroom, head over the toilet, when my roommate rushed in to get me. He was like, "What you been doing?"

I said, "I just feel sick." Luckily, it didn't go further than that.

After a while, though, I started to make myself hate food. I stopped eating breakfast and lunch altogether. It was hard; I was

Through Thick and Thin

hungry all the time. But I became accustomed to it.

I'm not fat anymore, but I fear ever being fat again. A few friends know about this, and they worry about me. They think it may have consequences, but so far I haven't seen any.

Still, since I started to write this story, I've begun to realize that I need to stop not eating. I've been getting a little better. I eat more—two meals instead of one.

The author was in high school when he wrote this story.

My Secret Habit

By Anonymous

When I was 15, I gained 20 lbs in a matter of months. The reason I gained so much weight so fast was simple. After breaking up with my boyfriend, I started eating like a pig. By May I looked like a total slob—and swimwear season was coming! I was miserable.

Meanwhile, my ex was parading around with his new girlfriend. Of course she was thin, which made me even more upset. But there was nothing I could do about it except continue stuffing my face.

One day, as I was drowning my sorrows in yet another pint of ice cream, I overheard my friend Cheryl (not her real name) talking to her cousin. Cheryl was thin, too. "It's so easy," she was saying. "Whenever you feel full, or when you feel guilty about eating pizza or"—she glanced at me—"ice cream, just go to the bathroom and throw up. You'll feel light again."

Her cousin and I stared at her in disgust. "That's stupid, Cheryl," I said. I thought, "You just can't throw up whenever you want."

Or can you?

The answer to my question came as soon as I finished dinner that night. Cheryl's words—"you'll feel light again"—stuck in my head as I went into the bathroom. I stared at the toilet for at least 10 minutes before I did anything. I leaned over the toilet bowl slowly, hearing the laughter coming from the living room, where my family was watching TV.

I stuck one finger down my throat. Nothing happened. I stuck a second, then a third, and then it all came rushing out of me. It was not the easiest thing in the world, but Cheryl was right. I felt light and empty, and I wasn't even hungry! My summer might not be that bad after all.

That's how I began my "little phase," as I like to call it. Every day, after dinner, I'd slip into the bathroom. I'd run the water in the tub so no one could hear what I was doing. Then I'd hurl away. The guilt I had about overeating left me along with the food.

After two weeks of this I looked at the scale. All I had lost was a ridiculous 4 lbs. Four pounds! I cried myself to sleep that night, fearing the worst—that I would be fat forever. Was that possible? With so many thin and beautiful women in the world, why couldn't I be like them?

I wasn't going to let myself stay fat and horrible so everyone could laugh at me. I started throwing up after every single meal, big or small, although most of them were huge. My "little habit" made it easier for me to eat all the food I wanted, because it would soon be gone anyway. I would eat five or six slices of pizza, sometimes more, plus ice cream by the ton, cookies, cakes, everything I could get my hands on. After each feast, I'd head for the bathroom.

After another two weeks, I looked at the scale again, and I'd lost 10 lbs! I was so happy, especially since everybody started paying me compliments about the way I looked. Cheryl was right. It was so easy.

Then, in late June, I noticed the bruises. Large black and blue marks were covering my arms and legs, and I had no idea how or why I was getting them. I also realized that I was in pain. My right side was killing me all the time and I had to lie down a lot. My period stopped for a while. And I started to have frequent bad dreams. I would wake up in a cold sweat, wondering what was happening to me. A slight fear would run through me, because I didn't know what was wrong, but at that point I didn't really care. I refused to accept that I had a problem. All I wanted was to be as thin as possible.

My "little habit" was affecting my personality as well as my body. I became extremely moody and irritable, and I would constantly yell at my brother and my mom. All I wanted was for them to leave me alone with my food. I would send my mom to the store to buy me something, then I'd eat and eat, and throw up before she got home. I had no social life, no hobbies. My life revolved around my obsession with food.

After dinner, I'd slip into the bathroom and run the water in the tub so no one could hear what I was doing.

Still, no one seemed to notice that anything was wrong with me. If they did, they didn't say anything. My friends noticed that I was going to the bathroom all the time, but I'd just make some excuse about being on a water diet.

In July, I heard the news: Cheryl was in the hospital. At first I thought she had an accident or something, but when I called her house, her brother told me the truth. Her mother caught her throwing up and dragged her to the hospital, kicking and screaming.

They found out that she had anorexia nervosa (a disorder in

which a person becomes so obsessed with dieting and thinness that she starves herself) and bulimia (when a person follows a pattern of eating a huge amount of food and then throwing up or taking laxatives to get rid of it). Cheryl's weight had dropped down to 85 lbs on a 5'7" frame, but her mom never realized her problem until she caught Cheryl in the act.

My mom went off when she found out. "I don't want you hanging around with that girl anymore! How could her mother not know what was wrong with her?" She continued ranting for about an hour, but I ignored her. My mom didn't realize I had the same problem as Cheryl, and now I knew not to tell her. She would kill me, and I would never hear the end of it.

I sat down and thought about what I was doing to myself, and what was happening to Cheryl. There was no comparison, I told myself. Her problem was way bigger than mine. But then I tried to remember: when was the last time that I ate a decent meal without throwing up afterwards? Almost four months ago. That's when I realized I had a serious problem. That day I decided to quit, because I didn't want to end up like Cheryl.

Stopping was much harder than starting had been. I still remember the first time I sat down to eat dinner after making my decision. Once it was over, I automatically got up to go to the bathroom, but I made myself sit down again. That was probably one of the hardest things I ever had to do.

I decided to go to the doctor, praying that my mother wouldn't have to know. Luckily, my doctor is a very understanding person. She counseled me and gave me a list of healthy things to eat. She gave me her phone number at home so I could call if I had any problems.

By the time I quit making myself throw up, I had lost almost 50 lbs (my goal when I started out was to lose 30). I know I've gained some of it back but I don't look at the scale anymore. My doctor tells me not to. No one really knows about my problem, except my doctor, and I'd like to keep it that way. I know my family and friends couldn't handle it.

It's been almost a year since I stopped, and I feel much better about myself now. My health is much better. I don't have as many mood swings. All the marks and the bad dreams are gone. And my social life is a lot better. Sometimes I still feel that I would like to lose more weight, but my thoughts go back to seeing Cheryl lying on that hospital bed.

After all I went through to have the "ideal body," I can now easily say that it wasn't worth the isolation and the pain. Being thin doesn't mean being happy.

The author was 17 when she wrote this story.
She later graduated from college with a degree in
English and journalism.

Traumatized by Eating

By Autumn Bush

My mother expected high achievements from my little sister and me. I wouldn't show her school papers with a grade any lower than 85%. I felt like she'd consider anything lower than that to be failing. I think it was because she had such high standards that I became a perfectionist, and not just in schoolwork. I had to take everything I did to a higher level in order to feel like it was good enough for my mother. When my family began teasing me about my weight, I took that to a higher level, too.

First, I stopped eating around people. Then I pretty much stopped eating altogether. By the time I realized I had an eating disorder, I could barely remember how to eat.

Around the time when I started trying not to eat much, my life looked good on the surface. I had lots of friends and was always the center of attention at school. But I had a lot of problems and I didn't feel like I could do anything about them.

For one, I was being sexually abused by a neighbor. I was afraid to tell anyone about the abuse, including my mother, because I thought they would blame me. I was also having problems with the teachers at my school. Maybe because I was being sexually abused, I felt that my teachers were too touchy. When they tried to touch me, even just to pat me on the shoulder and say I'd done a good job, I would snap at them and then get into trouble for it.

Not eating started as a way to avoid getting teased by my family, but it soon turned into a way to escape the problems that I didn't want to deal with, like the sexual abuse. Instead of worrying about the problems I couldn't control, I could just worry about what I had or hadn't eaten that day. At least I could control that.

It was hard to not eat lunch until I learned to fool myself into it. I'd tell myself that if I skipped lunch I would eat a whole lot of food when I got home. Then, at home, I learned to disregard my hunger. Gradually, my body adjusted to not having food, and that made me happy. It meant I was succeeding at my goal. If I had given in and started eating normally, I would not be dominating anything in my life. My life would have felt like a toy that was being controlled by other people.

I began to stop eating dinner as well as lunch. I figured that I could eat breakfast every morning, but I only ended up eating breakfast on Saturdays. At first, my energy was the same as it had always been, then I began to get a lot of headaches and stomachaches. Little by little, I began getting more sleep time than study time. I was not as focused on schoolwork as usual, but I somehow managed to maintain my grades. I didn't think any of it was because I was hurting my body. I thought that I only needed to get used to my new eating habits.

Though I didn't have much energy, I liked the way my body was looking. Other people began to notice and compliment my new, thinner figure, and I thought that I was finally getting some good attention. I was finally feeling like somebody.

In the middle of April, I told my guidance counselor that I was being sexually abused. Eventually, someone informed my mother, too. From what I heard, she said that it was not true, that I had not been sexually abused and that I was making it up for attention. That made me want to stop eating for the rest of my life.

In late October, I was scheduled to be moved to a foster home. I was hysterical, but there was no way for me to avoid it. Again, nothing was in my control. Even where I lived was not in my control. So I continued not eating.

My foster mother surprised me. She turned out to be a young individual with a young attitude. I immediately felt comfortable with her. Talking with her felt like visiting a relative.

> **By the time I realized I had an eating disorder, I could barely remember how to eat.**

Eventually, my foster mother began to notice that I was skipping dinner and spoke to me about not eating lunch. She tried to push me to eat a little more than I was. When I wouldn't, she told me that I had an eating disorder. At first, I denied it.

Then I began to talk to my guidance counselor about it. My guidance counselor told me where I could read more about eating disorders. I started researching eating disorders and found out that I was becoming an anorexic, someone who doesn't eat for long periods of time. I spoke with my foster mother about it, and she informed my social worker, who eventually got it to the ears of my mother.

Once again, my mother didn't pay any attention. She said I was just picky about what I ate. "You need to stop giving that girl so much attention," she said to my social worker. "You're filling her head up with nonsense. If you want her to eat, stop paying attention to her. She'll eat."

My social worker said, "I'll try your idea. You've known her longer."

I told myself I didn't care. If they thought that I was only doing it for attention, at least that would leave me in peace to continue not eating without being bothered. Luckily, my foster mother ignored my mother's advice, not me.

By then, I couldn't eat full meals. One chicken wing would make me full. I had lost 15 lbs and I looked like a twig. Before, I was known in my school as the girl with the big butt. Now people were noticing that my butt was not so big anymore. I went from having people tell me that they liked my new figure to them saying that I was not as appealing as I used to be. Friends told me that I looked sick.

I felt hurt and confused. When I first started losing weight, I had gotten the attention and approval I needed so much. But now that people thought that I had lost too much weight, I felt unwanted. I couldn't please anyone. Not even myself. I hated what was happening.

Sometimes I tried to eat, but since I had been not eating for so long, the food made me feel sick to my stomach and it would come right back up. This hurt me even more. I would lie awake at night crying, worrying that people were starting to hate me because of my eating habits. I was trying so hard to please everyone that it was breaking me down.

My foster mother was patient with me. She'd sit at the dinner table with me and not let me get up until I finished eating. I wanted to not eat, which gave me control, but I also wanted her approval, which I could only get through eating. So I learned how to get both.

I would eat. Then, when she wasn't really paying attention, I would go into the bathroom and throw up intentionally. I was moving from becoming an anorexic, someone who doesn't eat, to a bulimic, someone who purposefully throws up what she eats. I knew that I was developing a new eating disorder, and I did not feel good about it. My eating, the thing that gave me control, was starting to get out of my control. I was becoming a very sick teenager who could not cure this sickness. I needed help.

I began to read books on eating disorders. I learned that people can suffer long-term malnutrition or even die from what I was doing. I also learned that people who suffer from eating disorders are often perfectionists, like me. And many people with histories of sexual abuse, like me, develop eating disorders.

I decided to try to let people help me get better. But just thinking about doing that hurt. It felt like my eating disorder was forcing me to give over control to other people. I'd be falling into the mode of being controlled again.

> **My foster mother would sit at the dinner table with me and not let me get up until I finished eating.**

Despite my hurt feelings, I began working with my foster mother a little more. I began to eat three things on one plate at a time, and I told myself that I wouldn't throw up any of it.

It was hard because I still had the mentality that if I ate too much, I would gain a lot of weight. So then I would try to eat only a little. But the less I ate, the more I felt like I was falling back into being controlled by my eating disorder, and I wanted to get out of that. So little by little, I tried to make myself eat more than I felt comfortable eating. It was so hard. I worried that I'd gain a lot of weight and people wouldn't like me.

After I ate, it took a long time for the food to settle in my stomach and sometimes I just couldn't stand it. I would throw up the food even though I'd vowed not to. That made me feel bad. I didn't understand why I was still trying to eat if I was going to throw it back up.

But I kept working with my foster mother. I kept trying to eat and kept struggling with the uncomfortable feelings of wanting her approval and not wanting to feel like I was being controlled. As I worked with her, I began to notice other things in my life that I could control, which didn't hurt me, like the sports I played or the friends I kept. These were things that I would have never found out on my own. My foster mother helped me figure them out.

I still struggle with eating. Some days are easy, and I never even think about skipping meals. I just sit down and eat without thinking about it. On other days, I feel like I am battling the devil for my soul. The devil is my passion to have control. I could be really hungry, yet in my passion for control I try my hardest to fight off the hunger. On both the good and bad days, I try to pay attention to what I can control and what I cannot. Either I handle it on my own, or I speak to my foster mother about it.

I'm not sure what I'd have done without my foster mother to help me out. I know I'm very lucky to have someone in my life who I can trust to help me with my eating. She helped me broaden my horizons. Although every day is a struggle to continue eating, I think about the things that I would be giving up if I stopped eating. I would be hurting the people who love me as well as myself. Even though I sometimes become tempted to skip a meal, I try extra hard to help myself to the best of my ability. I hope it keeps becoming easier.

Autumn was 15 when she wrote this story.
She later graduated from Skidmore College.

Skinniest Man in the Graveyard

By Anonymous

I never gave my weight a second thought until I was 9, when my parents sent me to a summer camp in upstate New York for one month. All summer I listened to the kids insult me about my weight.

"We can't let you on the bus. You won't fit and we'll crash on our way."

"If you swim, you'll eat all the fish and drink the whole ocean."

I felt like crap when they teased me, and usually I made a joke to take attention away from my weight. Or I'd make excuses, saying, "I'm not really fat. I'm just working out right now and need the extra weight to turn it into muscle." When they didn't let up, I'd hit them with the hardest comeback I could, depending on what I knew about the kid who was teasing me, like: "Well, I'm not the one with no mom."

But sometimes I'd stay quiet, thinking, "He's right and I should be listening to him." I mean, I knew the kid was being mean, but I got the message loud and clear: being fat was unacceptable.

Today I know those kids who teased me were bullies, but back then I was so sad because I thought they were right. "How come I'm fat and I can't do anything about it?" I thought. "I should be doing something."

After summer camp, I started 4th grade believing I was the fat kid because I had the big stomach and the boobies. I hated it because the other guys, the thin ones, were always jumping around and hanging out with the girls. I was always left out and I thought it was because of my weight.

At my grandmother's house, seconds and another helping for home were a must.

Fortunately, I found some friends in my class who didn't judge kids who were different. They weren't fat, but they made me feel like my weight wasn't a problem.

But after school, I only thought about my weight. I weighed myself and looked at myself in the mirror three or four times a day. I used to walk on my toes around the house so I wouldn't hear how heavy I was when I walked. I'd lie down on my back and stretch really far, so it looked like I had no stomach at all.

In Eastern Europe, where I was born, bigger was always better and food was the center of the family. So I ate a lot at home. And the food was hearty, tangy and fulfilling. I especially loved my mom's special beef stroganoff recipe—strips of beef, beef stock, onions, mushrooms and ketchup. Let me tell you, the entire dish was always gone within two hours, all because of me.

My grandmother always believed that I was too skinny for my age. At her house, seconds and another helping for home were a must. The food was delicious and there was so much of it. I felt I was helping out by eating more so it didn't go to waste.

I don't want to put blame on everyone else, but the family food thing just overpowered me. And I've always liked more and more food, ever since I was a little kid. I felt that most people would put some food in their mouth and chew it over slowly, to get all the taste out of it. I shoveled: a little of this, a little of that, a little more and when the plate was empty, I got more. I ate food like I breathed air.

When I was 13, I looked at my scale and it said 134 lbs. I was only about 5' tall and I couldn't believe how enormous I was. I wasn't just fat. I was huge. It was right there under my nose.

I didn't understand why I was fat. I thought, "I was always so nice to so many people—why would God let me become so huge?" Of course he didn't answer me and I wondered what was wrong with me. Because of my weight, I felt ugly and lonely.

I didn't ask my parents for help with my weight, but I wish they had noticed and helped me do something about it. They could have helped me learn to stop when I was full so I wouldn't eat so much. If they'd only taken the food away from the table when we all had enough. But they didn't. When I was 14, my mom and dad just said, "Son, you've gained so much weight and you should lose it."

I eventually learned that there was a chart called the Body Mass Index (BMI), which showed you how much you should weigh depending on your height. I learned I was 50 lbs overweight for my height.

By the time I was 15, I decided it all had to go. I saw on TV that celebrities were losing weight by becoming bulimic or anorexic. I had no idea what that was, so I researched it online.

Then I starved myself as much as I possibly could. It's called anorexia and it was simple: you don't eat, so your body must eat itself (meaning its own fat, which I had plenty of).

I only did it for about three months, but oh man was I slimming down. I ate only bread and drank water every day, and I lost 40 lbs during that time. But my stomach felt as if a gremlin was inside and he was pushing and scratching at the walls to get out. Still, I loved the way I looked.

I also tried bulimia, which is essentially binge eating (overeating) followed by vomiting everything I'd just ingested. Once when I was 16, my grandma and I bought a huge amount of food at a Russian delicatessen. When it was all heated, I turned on the TV to *The Simpsons* and ate it all. Then I went into the bathroom, like I'd done so many times before, and blew it all out.

Throwing up was simple. Two fingers down the throat and out came all the crap that I regretted eating. But when I was done, it was disgusting. I smelled like throw up and my eyes were red from the pressure they'd just endured. I did it at least seven times a week.

Soon, I was throwing up almost all of my meals and I hated myself for it. I wanted to feel full and happy and eat things in moderate proportions.

Bulimia began to define me. I did it until I was so skinny that I thought I was beautiful.

But I didn't think I had the strength to lose weight slowly by eating right and exercising a little every day. My feelings about the weight I was losing overwhelmed my feelings about how I was doing it.

Bulimia began to define me, and I did it until I was so skinny that I thought I was beautiful. I used to look at myself in the mirror and I had no boobs and almost no stomach and everything was tight.

My parents thought it was great, but they didn't know how I was losing the weight. I lied to them and said I was simply exercising more often.

My parents never knew I was starving myself or throwing up my food, but I knew I couldn't practice bulimia for my entire life. I knew it would have killed me eventually.

So once I was happy with my weight, in the summer of my 16th year, I decided to stop throwing up. It was much easier to eat and sit than to eat and throw up. Of course, without controlling what or how much I ate, I couldn't keep the weight down. By the time I was 17, I'd gained all of it back.

Now that I'm 18 years old and living on my own, I've decided it's time to take control of my body and my diet. I'm 6' tall and I weigh 230 lbs. My ideal weight would be 175 (that's what I weighed when I was 16). That's 55 lbs to lose.

I know that to lose weight in a healthy way, I need to stay away from all the bad food out there. I could also eat slightly less when I do eat it. I could substitute sugary drinks with tea and water. And I've learned that things boiled or grilled are much healthier than frying. But I'm still not sure if I'm ready to change my eating and exercise habits to lose weight the right way.

When I was offered the opportunity to interview Dr. Melissa Nishawala, an eating disorders specialist at the NYU Child Study Center, I happily accepted. I knew I wasn't going to venture out on my own and find out the facts about eating disorders. I decided to interview the psychiatrist mostly for my personal benefit.

She told me that anorexia can actually cause the brain to shrink. It also causes the body to shut down the production of white blood cells, which fight infections in the body. Bulimia can reduce the amount of potassium in your body, which can affect your heart rhythm and can kill you. Throwing up also damages your stomach and esophagus and could lead to them rupturing.

When I asked her if either disease could kill you, she said, "Both can be deadly, absolutely—10% of people die, or maybe even more."

After talking to Dr. Nishawala, I decided that I'd never vomit or starve myself again. And I will warn people about the dangers of the disease. It's a self-inflicted disease and one of the dumbest things I ever did.

It wasn't that she gave me tips or ideas to stay healthy. It's that she convinced me that anorexia and bulimia would destroy me. And do I want that? No, I don't. I do not want to become the skinniest man in the graveyard.

The author was 18 when he wrote this story.

Melissa 'Piccolo' Rivera

Sticks and Stones

By Anne Ueland

Looking in the mirror, all I see is ugliness. This is how I have felt for the past seven years. In 4th grade, girls in my class used to pick on me, saying things like, "She is nasty," or, "She stinks." They also talked about my weight and made fun of me while I ate. That made me feel real bad. The only thing that I wanted to do when they said these things was go home, watch TV, and eat everything in sight.

Today, if someone walks by me and they smell bad, I might laugh. But I try not to, because I think back to when that was happening to me, and I remember how bad it felt and how hard my life was.

See, growing up with my parents was very lonely for me. They never paid me much attention. They did not teach me about keeping myself clean. The only friends that I seemed to have were the TV, swimming, basketball, and food.

But the more I ate and the worse I smelled, the more people talked bad about me and the more I looked at myself and saw ugliness. Days would go by that I would hate to look at myself in the mirror. I hated everything about myself. I felt like a complete failure.

It wasn't just people at school saying bad things about me. My mother used to always compare me to other people. She always said this one girl named Nancy looked better than I did. She used to say how Nancy had a brighter face than mine. She would even say things like, "Why can't you be more like Nancy?" She would always say that I was crazy or that I was a good-for-nothing. My mother even used to say that she wished I were never born.

Also, my parents never cooked anything for me, so I only had junk food to eat. I used to eat bags of chips and about a carton of ice cream a day. Junk food and TV made me feel better. It made me forget some of the things people said about me.

But soon my mother was getting upset about me eating all the food in the house. She started hiding the food so I had nothing to eat at all. She also said that I was a fat pig. That comment really hurt me, and I took it to heart. I felt so ashamed of the way I looked. I decided I would lose weight, because I wanted the kids at school to stop talking about me. Plus, I wanted my mother to stop calling me a fat pig. So when food was around, I tried not to eat as much of it. It worked. I began losing weight.

I also started learning about personal hygiene. When I was in 6th grade, one of my teachers taught a lesson about taking care of yourself. She taught us that a person needs to wash every day to have good hygiene. I started washing every day and I began to see the results in the way people treated me. The girls in my class started talking to me more, and talking less mess about me. But I was still unhappy. I had lost weight, but nothing seemed to help what was happening at home. My mother still put me down and said that I was never going to make it in life, and I believed her.

Finally, after being abused for a long time, I was placed in the foster care system at the age of 12. I started to feel a little better about myself because I was not hearing my mother's criticisms of me. Some days I would look in the mirror and feel fine about myself. But other days I would look and see the fat pig that my mother was talking about. I saw the ugliness my mother saw in me.

To try to ease the pain that I felt and to have some control over my weight, I stopped eating completely. I even ended up in the hospital for a while because I got so frail. I weighed only 100 lbs. Sometimes when I looked in the mirror, I could tell that I was really damaging my body. I looked too thin. Other times, I saw that ugly, fat pig. Those times I really did not want to eat much of anything.

I wanted the kids at school to stop talking about me. I wanted my mother to stop calling me a fat pig.

Soon after leaving the hospital I was moved to a new group home. While I was there, I didn't see much of my mother. In a way it was good, because I didn't hear her criticisms and I started to feel a little better, but I also missed her. After all, she is my mother. Soon I was allowed home visits.

The first day I stayed at her house I started to feel real bad about myself all over again. Right away she called me all kinds of names, like a tramp and a ho. Home visits after that weren't easier. When I got allowance from the group home, she said I got the money from sleeping with guys. My mother even had a special cup for me to drink out of because she said that I was sucking d-cks. She also used to say that I had a bunch of sexually transmitted diseases.

I knew that what my mother was saying was not true, but it still hurt me a lot to hear it. At the time, I was not even having sex. Days and nights would go by when I would cry about the things she said.

My social worker and the staff at my house would tell my

mother that I was doing well, but she never believed them. I wanted her to know that I was doing well; I wanted us to be close, but every time I saw her she just said bad things to me.

To this day it's still hard for me to figure out how to have a relationship with my mother. She is my only living relative, and I want her in my life. But the things she says push me away instead of making us closer. Though I can now recognize that things she says about me aren't true, they still make me feel really bad about myself.

When people joke with me and say I'm fat—even when what they really mean is that I'm very thin—it makes me feel bad. It reminds me of the girls who were mean to me at school and my mother's criticisms of me. I hope that one day I will reach the point where I feel comfortable enough with who I am and the way I look that what people say won't affect me so much.

Anne was 19 when she wrote this story.

Finding My Way Home

By Aquellah Mahdi

The first time I remember having issues with eating was after a comment my dad made. I forget how old I was, but I remember his words like it was yesterday. He said, "If you keep eating like that you will end up looking like your mother."

To me, that meant I'd end up fat and couch-bound with no one to love me. At the time, my father was sexually abusing me and my mother was letting it happen. When my dad made that comment I felt like he was a fortune-teller. He was reading my future and my body was his concern.

After that, I changed my eating habits in lots of small ways. I began to limit the amount I would place on my plate compared to my mom. Sometimes I would skip meals, and it was around this time that I had my first few laxatives.

When I was 13 I lost a lot of weight. I began to go out for daily runs, and I started to do a lot of sit-ups and push-ups, even lifting phone books to reduce the fat in my arms. At first, I was just trying to stop my depression about what was going on at home.

Controlling my weight gave me some stability. If my mom started her speech about me stealing her husband away, I couldn't speak back because of my fear of being punished by her and then by my dad. Instead, I'd go into my room and do sit-ups or spit out my food. It was like getting back at them both. Only they didn't notice I was deteriorating.

When I finally told my godmother about the abuse, my twin sister and I were put in foster care.

My struggles with eating went up and down for the next couple of years. I'd eat for a few days, then go on what I called my fasting period. At times I had a normal appetite. But when certain fatty foods were placed in front of me, I'd say to myself, "Think of how many calories you're about to eat," or, "Look at the amount your sister has on her plate. You're going to be the fat twin." I wanted and needed to keep myself the slender one, the one who might not be as smart but who had the better body, the most self-discipline.

Moving from one home to the next made it easy to cover up what I was doing. No one took the time out to notice what was going on, and somehow I enjoyed that. My eating disorder was a secret I could keep to myself.

When I was 16 I moved to a group home and my eating disorder became full-blown. I think it was the freedom of making my own plate of food. I could put any amount I wanted on the plate and no one could say anything.

I started to count calories whenever I had the chance. Restricting myself to 500 calories a day or less was like a treat. Later I could burn off all the fat that I had put on in a day, plus one pound more. I had started binging and purging (eating a lot and then throwing it up) and abusing laxatives. I used diet pills when I wanted to. No one knew anything. I was in charge of what went into my body and how it was going to come out.

Through Thick and Thin

I didn't think what I was doing was a problem. Controlling my weight was my only chance to hold on to something that felt real. I needed to feel alive.

This went on for a few years, until I moved in with Yolanda, my current foster mom. Yolanda's love and support from the day I walked into her home helped me feel like it was OK to tell her anything. I had never told anyone about my eating disorder, but I told Yolanda.

After a few months of living with her, I wanted, for the very first time in four years, to get some real help for my problem. I hated to see and hear Yolanda's concerns about my deteriorating health. I wasn't used to someone noticing what I was doing to my body. When she said it was time that I got some help that I should have gotten a while ago, I said to myself, "It's time for a change."

I started going to group therapy, hoping it would make me feel more comfortable communicating with others about what I was struggling with. At the group leader's suggestion, I started to see a nutritional therapist.

We set up some goals for my first week, like if I skipped a meal I would have a small snack instead. I would also have to try to cut back on exercise and purging.

I knew that would be really hard for me. After just one small meal I'd see myself in the mirror weighing in at 250 lbs, and I'd do about 400 sit-ups in my bed. I was abusing laxatives daily. I'd run in place in the shower and sleep with plastic bags wrapped around my thighs to burn off extra calories. I even ate Ajax to help curb my appetite.

As I tried to slow this behavior down, I began to clean like a maniac and worry about my calories all the time. I was afraid to go into the supermarket. I thought I would get fat just from looking at all the food.

I tried some coping skills, like this technique my therapist taught me: When you are having a rough time, you imagine a stream, and every leaf that goes by has a feeling that you feel on it. The stream washes your feelings away. This helped me when I ate. I thought of how every bite was being washed away.

Some other things that helped were drawing pictures, Rollerblading and shopping. I'd give myself a reward each time I went an entire day without criticizing my body or skipping a meal.

But of course there were things that just made it difficult to stick to my coping skills and my meal plans. Things like negative thinking (telling myself I'm fat or stupid) and anger about the abuse I'd suffered.

I struggled with inner confusion about eating. If I ate this much, was I going to look just like my mother or my sister? I'd remember the words of my dad: "If you eat that you will start to look just like your mother." My thoughts were in limbo. Was I already like her? Did my dad do all of those things to me because of my weight?

I was in charge of what went into my body and how it was going to come out.

I constantly thought about my illness and my past and wondered if there was some kind of connection. Even if there wasn't, I wanted to be assured that whatever I was feeling was OK. I needed that comfort. I needed a professional to assure me that my eating disorder wasn't just because of the media or the websites I looked at, that my past traumas still play a huge role in my disorder.

But I couldn't speak up about the things that were bothering me. "I'm fine," was the phrase I used to start a conversation and end it. Later, I'd sit by myself and think of the chance I'd had to open up to someone and didn't. I kept putting up this wall toward anyone who tried to help me, and we never got anywhere.

All of the attempts I made—the private treatment, the groups—seemed to work for me at the time. But then Ed (as I called my eating disorder) would get the last few words in the decision. It was always back to square one.

I started to have heart problems and I became dehydrated. My hair started to fall out and my teeth became eroded. Yolanda would constantly tell me, "Thin is not in. You look sick in your face." I guess my mind changed one day while I was outside skating. I started to get some pains in my chest. It freaked me out. I never want to experience that again.

It was time to go inpatient. That was everyone's decision, all the members of my treatment team. Even me. I felt like it was time to stop the games and beat Ed.

On August 28, 2006 I continued my journey on the path to recovery. I was admitted inpatient to The Renfrew Center in Philadelphia. When I first came to the center I thought, "Wow! This looks a lot like a college." There was something here that was different from any of my other treatments.

We had welcomed this disease into our lives, and now we had to learn to say goodbye.

I was surrounded by so many people, mostly women and teenage girls. My first impression was that I wasn't as small as many of them and that I didn't need as much help as they did. After a few days I came to see that we were all in the same place in our lives. All of us were struggling with the same disease. Every day was a challenge.

Everyone in treatment was doing a lot of work to get better. People had spent five to even 30 years struggling with this disorder. I started to feel like I didn't have to hide behind Ed. I could look the disorder in the face and tell it that I needed to take control now. This was my cue. If I was ever going to get my chance to try and start to heal it was going to be there at The Renfrew Center.

The days at Renfrew were hard. To most people, meals are

not a big deal, but to me they were so huge. During meals everyone was supportive. No talk of calories, past treatment or meal plans was allowed. After meals there was always a support group where I could tell everyone how it went and how I was feeling.

Groups on different topics ran all day. Each one brought me one step closer to healing inside and out. Art was my favorite because I didn't have to speak much, just put my feelings into art and then explain what I'd created.

I created a doll to represent my inner child. I gave her closure from the abuse and protected her from Ed. I let her speak her story to my therapist through letters. I wrote and she came out. We worked to let her feel love and life. I can never give her back her childhood, but I could give her a hug, and when I told her it wasn't her fault, the world lifted off of her shoulders.

My therapist at Renfrew played a huge role in my recovery. She saw it as an honor to embark on this journey with me. She taught me techniques to keep me focused and in the moment, like putting my hands in a bowl of ice. It may sound weird, but it helped me keep my body in the present so I would remain mindful of my feelings.

Then there were the residents. Each helped me in a different way, to finish off my last bite or let me be a part of their family activity during visiting hours, so I wouldn't feel so lonely on the weekends. With their help I was never alone.

What kept us all connected was that we had befriended this disease. We had welcomed it into our lives, and now we had to learn to say goodbye.

On October 20, 2006 I left The Renfrew Center. I think the day before I was discharged was the hardest for me. I had to say goodbye to my therapist, to the young women who had accepted me into their families and to the staff members who helped me through all of the bad nights. What would I do without all of them in my life?

As the car was driving away from the place where I'd spent

my five weeks fighting this demon called Ed, all I could do was sit in the backseat and tell myself: "Just do the things you practiced here; you can still beat Ed." With that in mind I let go of my fear, took a deep breath and turned my head straight to the road ahead of me. I began my journey home.

*Aquellah was 20 when she wrote this story.
She enrolled in college to study nursing and art therapy.*

Recovering From an Eating Disorder

Mary Hopper, MA, is a primary therapist on the adolescent team at The Renfrew Center, a research and inpatient treatment center for people with eating disorders. She answered our questions on how to recover.

Q: Why do people develop eating disorders?
A: It's complicated, and it's different for everyone. But in general, eating disorders appear to be a way to cope with feelings that feel intolerable. Things like abandonment, hurt, sadness, anger, fear and so on. It can stem from trauma, because traumatic memories are horrible and no wants to feel them or deal with them. An eating disorder keeps you so preoccupied, it's so consuming, that it helps you not have to remember stuff from your past that's traumatic.

Manipulating food, and your weight, is a way of rescuing yourself from having to feel anything. Being able to focus on all this stuff (when to eat, how much, when to throw up) is like a full-time job. It helps distract you from all the things in your life you can't control. It can even be physically numbing, and certainly it emotionally numbs the person

Also, eating disorders can be a way of wanting, usually unconsciously, to show people how bad you feel on the inside. Maybe you can't talk about it, or no one is listening. But if you make yourself look like a skeleton, people are going to pay attention.

Q: What does it take to recover?

A: You really need a treatment team: a nutritionist, a psychiatrist to help with medications, a therapist to help you identify what needs you're trying to get met by using the disorder, and a family therapist to help parents or siblings really listen and try to make changes so you don't feel so alone.

Q: What are the first steps?

A: You first have to learn how to keep yourself safe: by eating, following your meal plan and taking care of your body. Then you can focus on what was causing these behaviors.

If you're still restricting and binging and purging, you can't engage with anything, because you can't feel anything. That's what's great about inpatient treatment: there is all this attention paid to making sure you are eating, so then you can start feeling and doing the emotional work.

Q: How long does it take?

A: Once you decide that you want to get better, it can take between three and seven years to fully recover. You're really changing a lifestyle pattern you've had for years. Eating disorders don't happen overnight. They're usually a culmination of many years of pain and suffering. To recover, you need to change how you relate, and the way you deal with conflict or sadness, as well handling the changes in your body. It takes ongoing therapy.

The good news is our experience shows that if patients are committed, their symptoms will not be as severe all the way through. It will get easier.

Q: How do you know you're really recovered?

A: Some people feel that with an eating disorder, like with an alcohol or drug addiction, you can never consider yourself fully recovered. Because an eating disorder is a response to intense feelings, someone might be fine for 10 years, then a trauma happens and they'll return to the disorder. Usually it's brief, and not as severe as it was originally, but that's why it's hard to say someone is recovered.

You can't recover alone. The more support you get from the more people, the better you're going to do.

One way to keep yourself safe is with therapy. Eating disorders are fueled by unconscious stuff. Therapy is a way of helping the unconscious become conscious, making you aware of what your issues are so you can do something about them.

Q: How can you manage your recovery once you leave a supportive environment like Renfrew?

A: What we find works best is that after a patient leaves an inpatient center, they should gradually step down first to a day treatment program (where you live at home but attend every day for most of the day) and then to less intensive outpatient programs.

Often, people with eating disorders think they can do everything alone. But you can't recover alone. You really need your family, your friends and a treatment team. The more support you get from the more people, the better you're going to do.

For more information, visit www.renfrewcenter.com or call 1-800-RENFREW. You can ask questions and get advice from others in recovery at www.RUhungry.org.

Additional Resources:

Eating Disorders Awareness and Prevention (EDAP)
1-800-931-2237
www.nationaleatingdisorders.org

National Association of Anorexia Nervosa and Associated Disorders (ANAD)
847-831-3438
www.anad.org

Overeater's Anonymous
505-891-2664
www.overeatersanonymous.org

FICTION SPECIAL

Lost and Found

Darcy Wills winced at the loud rap music coming from her sister's room.

My rhymes were rockin'
MC's were droppin'
People shoutin' and hip-hoppin'
Step to me and you'll be inferior
'Cause I'm your lyrical superior.

Darcy went to Grandma's room. The darkened room smelled of lilac perfume, Grandma's favorite, but since her stroke Grandma did not notice it, or much of anything.

"Bye, Grandma," Darcy whispered from the doorway. "I'm going to school now."

Just then, the music from Jamee's room cut off, and Jamee rushed into the hallway.

The teen characters in the Bluford novels, a fiction series by Townsend Press, struggle with many of the same difficult issues as the writers in this book. This is the first chapter from *Lost and Found*, by Anne Scraff, the first book in the series. In this novel, high school sophomore Darcy contends with the return of her long-absent father, the troubling behavior of her younger sister Jamee, and the beginning of her first relationship.

"Like she even hears you," Jamee said as she passed Darcy. Just two years younger than Darcy, Jamee was in eighth grade, though she looked older.

"It's still nice to talk to her. Sometimes she understands. You want to pretend she's not here or something?"

"She's not," Jamee said, grabbing her backpack.

"Did you study for your math test?" Darcy asked. Mom was an emergency room nurse who worked rotating shifts. Most of the time, Mom was too tired to pay much attention to the girls' schoolwork. So Darcy tried to keep track of Jamee.

"Mind your own business," Jamee snapped.

"You got two D's on your last report card," Darcy scolded. "You wanna flunk?" Darcy did not want to sound like a nagging parent, but Jamee wasn't doing her best. Maybe she couldn't make A's like Darcy, but she could do better.

Jamee stomped out of the apartment, slamming the door behind her. "Mom's trying to get some rest!" Darcy yelled. "Do you have to be so selfish?" But Jamee was already gone, and the apartment was suddenly quiet.

Darcy loved her sister. Once, they had been good friends. But now all Jamee cared about was her new group of rowdy friends. They leaned on cars outside of school and turned up rap music on their boom boxes until the street seemed to tremble like an earthquake. Jamee had even stopped hanging out with her old friend Alisha Wrobel, something she used to do every weekend.

Darcy went back into the living room, where her mother sat in the recliner sipping coffee. "I'll be home at 2:30, Mom," Darcy said. Mom smiled faintly. She was tired, always tired. And lately she was worried too. The hospital where she worked was cutting staff. It seemed each day fewer people were expected to do more work. It was like trying to climb a mountain that keeps getting taller as you go. Mom was forty-four, but just yesterday she said, "I'm like an old car that's run out of warranty, baby. You know what happens then. Old car is ready for the junk heap. Well, maybe that hospital is gonna tell me one of these days—'Mattie Mae Wills, we don't need you anymore. We can get somebody younger and cheaper.'"

"Mom, you're not old at all," Darcy had said, but they were only words, empty words. They could not erase the dark, weary lines from beneath her mother's eyes.

Darcy headed down the street toward Bluford High School. It was not a terrible neighborhood they lived in; it just was not good. Many front yards were not cared for. Debris—fast food wrappers, plastic bags, old newspapers—blew around and piled against fences and curbs. Darcy hated that. Sometimes she and other kids from school spent Saturday mornings cleaning up, but it seemed a losing battle. Now, as she walked, she tried to focus on small spots of beauty along the way. Mrs. Walker's pink and white roses bobbed proudly in the morning breeze. The Hustons' rock garden was carefully designed around a wooden windmill.

As she neared Bluford, Darcy thought about the science project that her biology teacher, Ms. Reed, was assigning. Darcy was doing hers on tidal pools. She was looking forward to visiting a real tidal pool, taking pictures, and doing research. Today, Ms. Reed would be dividing the students into teams of two. Darcy wanted to be paired with her close friend, Brisana Meeks. They were both excellent students, a cut above most kids at Bluford, Darcy thought.

"Today, we are forming project teams so that each student can gain something valuable from the other," Ms. Reed said as Darcy sat at her desk. Ms. Reed was a tall, stately woman who reminded Darcy of the Statue of Liberty. She would have been a perfect model for the statue if Lady Liberty had been a black woman. She never would have been called pretty, but it was possible she might have been called a handsome woman. "For this assignment, each of you will be working with someone you've never worked with before."

Darcy was worried. If she was not teamed with Brisana,

maybe she would be teamed with some really dumb student who would pull her down. Darcy was a little ashamed of herself for thinking that way. Grandma used to say that all flowers are equal, but different. The simple daisy was just as lovely as the prize rose. But still Darcy did not want to be paired with some weak partner who would lower her grade.

"Darcy Wills will be teamed with Tarah Carson," Ms. Reed announced.

Darcy gasped. Not Tarah! Not that big, chunky girl with the brassy voice who squeezed herself into tight skirts and wore lime green or hot pink satin tops and cheap jewelry. Not Tarah who hung out with Cooper Hodden, that loser who was barely hanging on to his football eligibility. Darcy had heard that Cooper had been left back once or twice and even got his driver's license as a sophomore. Darcy's face felt hot with anger. Why was Ms. Reed doing this?

Hakeem Randall, a handsome, shy boy who sat in the back row, was teamed with the class blabbermouth, LaShawn Appleby. Darcy had a secret crush on Hakeem since freshman year. So far she had only shared this with her diary, never with another living soul.

It was almost as though Ms. Reed was playing some devilish game. Darcy glanced at Tarah, who was smiling broadly. Tarah had an enormous smile, and her teeth contrasted harshly with her dark red lipstick. "Great," Darcy muttered under her breath.

Ms. Reed ord e red the teams to meet so they could begin to plan their projects.

As she sat down by Tarah, Darcy was instantly sickened by a syrupy-sweet odor.

She must have doused herself with cheap perfume this morning, Darcy thought.

"Hey, girl," Tarah said. "Well, don't you look down in the mouth. What's got you lookin' that way?"

It was hard for Darcy to meet new people, especially some-

Lost and Found

one like Tarah, a person Aunt Charlotte would call "low class." These were people who were loud and rude. They drank too much, used drugs, got into fights and ruined the neighborhood. They yelled ugly insults at people, even at their friends. Darcy did not actually know that Tarah did anything like this personally, but she seemed like the type who did.

"I just didn't think you'd be interested in tidal pools," Darcy explained.

Tarah slammed her big hand on the desk, making her gold bracelets jangle like ice cubes in a glass, and laughed. Darcy had never heard a mule bray, but she was sure it made exactly the same sound. Then Tarah leaned close and whispered, "Girl, I don't know a tidal pool from a fool. Ms. Reed stuck us together to mess with our heads, you hear what I'm sayin'?"

"Maybe we could switch to other partners," Darcy said nervously.

A big smile spread slowly over Tarah's face. "Nah, I think I'm gonna enjoy this. You're always sittin' here like a princess collecting your A's. Now you gotta work with a regular person, so you better loosen up, girl!"

Darcy felt as if her teeth were glued to her tongue. She fumbled in her bag for her outline of the project. It all seemed like a horrible joke now. She and Tarah Carson standing knee-deep in the muck of a tidal pool!

"Worms live there, don't they?" Tarah asked, twisting a big gold ring on her chubby finger.

"Yeah, I guess," Darcy replied.

"Big green worms," Tarah continued. "So if you get your feet stuck in the bottom of that old tidal pool, and you can't get out, do the worms crawl up your clothes?"

Darcy ignored the remark. "I'd like for us to go there soon, you know, look around."

"My boyfriend, Cooper, he goes down to the ocean all the time. He can take us. He says he's seen these fiddler crabs. They look like big spiders, and they'll try to bite your toes off. Cooper says so," Tarah said.

"Stop being silly," Darcy shot back. "If you' re not even going to be serious . . . "

"You think you're better than me, don't you?" Tarah suddenly growled.

"I never said—" Darcy blurted.

"You don't have to say it, girl. It's in your eyes. You think I'm a low-life and you're something special. Well, I got more friends than you got fingers and toes together. You got no friends, and everybody laughs at you behind your back. Know what the word on you is? Darcy Wills give you the chills."

Just then, the bell rang, and Darcy was glad for the excuse to turn away from Tarah, to hide the hot tears welling in her eyes. She quickly rushed from the classroom, relieved that school was over. Darcy did not think she could bear to sit through another class just now.

Darcy headed down the long street towards home. She did not like Tarah . Maybe it was wrong, but it was true. Still, Tarah's brutal words hurt. Even stupid, awful people might tell you the truth about yourself. And Darcy did not have any real friends, except for Brisana. Maybe the other kids were mocking her behind her back. Darcy was very slender, not as shapely as many of the other girls. She remembered the time when Cooper Hodden was hanging in front of the deli with his friends, and he yelled as Darcy went by, "Hey, is that really a female there? Sure don't look like it. Looks more like an old broomstick with hair. " His companions laughed rudely, and Darcy had walked a little faster.

A terrible thought clawed at Darcy. Maybe she was the loser, not Tarah. Tarah was always hanging with a bunch of kids, laughing and joking. She would go down the hall to the lockers and greetings would come from everywhere. "Hey, Tarah!" "What's up, Tar?" "See ya at lunch, girl." When Darcy went to the lockers, there was dead silence.

Darcy usually glanced into stores on her way home from school. She enjoyed looking at the trays of chicken feet and pork ears at the little Asian grocery store. Sometimes she would even steal a glance at the diners sitting by the picture window at the Golden Grill Restaurant. But today she stare d straight ahead, her shoulders drooping.

If this had happened last year, she would have gone directly to Grandma's house, a block from where Darcy lived. How many times had Darcy and Jamee run to Grandma's, eaten applesauce cookies, drunk cider, and poured out their troubles to Grandma. Somehow, their problems would always dissolve in the warmth of her love and wisdom. But now Grandma was a frail figure in the corner of their apartment, saying little. And what little she did say made less and less sense.

Darcy was usually the first one home. The minute she got there, Mom left for the hospital to take the 3:00 to 11:00 shift in the ER. By the time Mom finished her paperwork at the hospital, she would be lucky to be home again by midnight. After Mom left, Darcy went to Grandma's room to give her the malted nutrition drink that the doctor ordered her to have three times a day.

"Want to drink your chocolate malt, Grandma?" Darcy asked, pulling up a chair beside Grandma's bed.

Grandma was sitting up, and her eyes were open. "No. I'm not hungry," she said listlessly. She always said that.

"You need to drink your malt, Grandma," Darcy insisted, gently putting the straw between the pinched lips.

Grandma sucked the malt slowly. "Grandma, nobody likes me at school," Darcy said. She did not expect any response. But there was a strange comfort in telling Grandma anyway. "Everybody laughs at me. It's because I'm shy and maybe stuck-up, too, I guess. But I don't mean to be. Stuck-up, I mean. Maybe I'm weird. I could be weird, I guess. I could be like Aunt Charlotte . . ." Tears rolled down Darcy's cheeks. Her heart ached with loneliness. There was nobody to talk to anymore, nobody who had time to listen, nobody who understood.

Grandma blinked and pushed the straw away. Her eyes brightened as they did now and then. "You are a wonderful girl. Everybody knows that," Grandma said in an almost normal voice. It happened like that sometimes. It was like being in the middle of a dark storm and having the clouds part, revealing a patch of clear, sunlit blue. For just a few precious minutes, Grandma was bright-eyed and saying normal things.

"Oh, Grandma, I'm so lonely," Darcy cried, pressing her head against Grandma's small shoulder.

"You were such a beautiful baby," Grandma said, stroking her hair." 'That one is going to shine like the morning star.' That's what I told your Mama. 'That child is going to shine like the morning star.' Tell me, Angelcake, is your daddy home yet?"

Darcy straightened. "Not yet." Her heart pounded so hard, she could feel it thumping in her chest. Darcy's father had not been home in five years.

"Well, tell him to see me when he gets home. I want him to buy you that blue dress you liked in the store window. That's for you, Angelcake. Tell him I've got money. My social security came, you know. I have money for the blue dress," Grandma said, her eyes slipping shut.

Just then, Darcy heard the apartment door slam. Jamee had come home. Now she stood in the hall, her hands belligerently on her hips. "Are you talking to Grandma again?" Jamee demanded.

"She was talking like normal," Darcy said. "Sometimes she does. You know she does."

"That is so stupid," Jamee snapped. "She never says anything right anymore. Not anything!" Jamee's voice trembled.

Darcy got up quickly and set down the can of malted milk. She ran to Jamee and put her arms around her sister. "Jamee, I know you're hurting too."

"Oh, don't be stupid," Jamee protested, but Darcy hugged her more tightly, and in a few seconds Jamee was crying. "She was the best thing in this stupid house," Jamee cried. "Why'd she have to go?"

"She didn't go," Darcy said. "Not really."

"She did! She did!" Jamee sobbed. She struggled free of Darcy, ran to her room, and slammed the door. In a minute, Darcy heard the bone-rattling sound of rap music.

Lost and Found, *a Bluford Series*™ *novel, is reprinted with permission from Townsend Press. Copyright © 2002.*

Want to read more? This and other *Bluford Series*™ novels and paperbacks can be purchased for $1 each at www.townsendpress.com.

Teens:
How to Get More Out of This Book

Self-help: The teens who wrote the stories in this book did so because they hope that telling their stories will help readers who are facing similar challenges. They want you to know that you are not alone, and that taking specific steps can help you manage or overcome very difficult situations. They've done their best to be clear about the actions that worked for them so you can see if they'll work for you.

Writing: You can also use the book to improve your writing skills. Each teen in this book wrote 5-10 drafts of his or her story before it was published. If you read the stories closely you'll see that the teens work to include a beginning, a middle, and an end, and good scenes, description, dialogue, and anecdotes (little stories). To improve your writing, take a look at how these writers construct their stories. Try some of their techniques in your own writing.

Reading: Finally, you'll notice that we include the first chapter from a Bluford Series novel in this book, alongside the true stories by teens. We hope you'll like it enough to continue reading. The more you read, the more you'll strengthen your reading skills. Teens at Youth Communication like the Bluford novels because they explore themes similar to those in their own stories. Your school may already have the Bluford books. If not, you can order them online for only $1.

Resources on the Web

We will occasionally post Think About It questions on our website, www.youthcomm.org, to accompany stories in this and other Youth Communication books. We try out the questions with teens and post the ones they like best. Many teens report that writing answers to those questions in a journal is very helpful.

How to Use This Book in Staff Training

Staff say that reading these stories gives them greater insight into what teens are thinking and feeling, and new strategies for working with them. You can help the staff you work with by using these stories as case studies.

Select one story to read in the group, and ask staff to identify and discuss the main issue facing the teen. There may be disagreement about this, based on the background and experience of staff. That is fine. One point of the exercise is that teens have complex lives and needs. Adults can probably be more effective if they don't focus too narrowly and can see several dimensions of their clients.

Ask staff: What issues or feelings does the story provoke in them? What kind of help do they think the teen wants? What interventions are likely to be most promising? Least effective? Why? How would you build trust with the teen writer? How have other adults failed the teen, and how might that affect his or her willingness to accept help? What other resources would be helpful to this teen, such as peer support, a mentor, counseling, family therapy, etc.

Resources on the Web

From time to time we will post Think About It questions on our website, www.youthcomm.org, to accompany stories in this and other Youth Communication books. We try out the questions with teens and post the ones that they find most effective. We'll also post lesson for some of the stories. Adults can use the questions and lessons in workshops.

> **Discussion Guide**

Teachers and Staff:
How to Use This Book in Groups

When working with teens individually or in groups, using these stories can help young people face difficult issues in a way that feels safe to them. That's because talking about the issues in the stories usually feels safer to teens than talking about those same issues in their own lives. Addressing issues through the stories allows for some personal distance; they hit close to home, but not too close. Talking about them opens up a safe place for reflection. As teens gain confidence talking about the issues in the stories, they usually become more comfortable talking about those issues in their own lives.

Below are general questions that can help you lead discussions about the stories, which help teens and staff reflect on the issues in their own work and lives. In most cases you can read a story and conduct a discussion in one 45-minute session. Teens are usually happy to read the stories aloud, with each teen reading a paragraph or two. (Allow teens to pass if they don't want to read.) It takes 10-15 minutes to read a story straight through. However, it is often more effective to let workshop participants make comments and discuss the story as you go along. The workshop leader may even want to annotate her copy of the story beforehand with key questions.

If teens read the story ahead of time or silently, it's good to break the ice with a few questions that get everyone on the same page: Who is the main character? How old is she? What happened to her? How did she respond? Etc. Another good starting question is: "What stood out for you in the story?" Go around the room and let each person briefly mention one thing.

Then move on to open-ended questions, which encourage participants to think more deeply about what the writers were feeling, the choices they faced, and they actions they took. There are no right or wrong answers to the open-ended questions. Open-ended questions encourage participants to think about how the themes, emotions and choices in the stories relate to their own lives. Here are some examples of open-ended questions that we have found to be effective. You can use variations of these questions with almost any story in this book.

—What main problem or challenge did the writer face?

—What choices did the teen have in trying to deal with the problem?

—Which way of dealing with the problem was most effective for the teen? Why?

—What strengths, skills, or resources did the teen use to address the challenge?

—If you were in the writer's shoes, what would you have done?

—What could adults have done better to help this young person?

—What have you learned by reading this story that you didn't know before?

—What, if anything, will you do differently after reading this story?

—What surprised you in this story?

—Do you have a different view of this issue, or see a different way of dealing with it, after reading this story? Why or why not?

Credits

The stories in this book all appeared in the following Youth Communication publications:

"Addicted to Food," by Miguel Ayala, *Represent*, September/October 2003

"Lighten Up On Heavy People," by Jennifer Cuttino, *New Youth Connections*, December 1990

"Scaling Back," by Erica Harrigan, *Represent*, January/February 2005

"Shapin' Up!" by Antwaun Garcia, *Represent*, September/October 2003

"My Body Betrayed Me," by Christine M., *Represent*, September/October 2003

"Big, Black, and Beautiful," by Anonymous, *New Youth Connections*, December 1997

"How I Overcame Being Overweight," by Shaniqua Sockwell, *Represent*, July/August 1996

"Are Teens Getting Too Fat?" by Megan Cohen, *New Youth Connections*, December 2004

"The War of the Weights," by Elizabeth Thompson, *New Youth Connections*, April 1998

"Naturally Thin," by Desiree Guery, *New Youth Connections*, September/October 2002

"Overboard With Exercise," by Shavone Harris, *New Youth Connections*, December 2000

"I Took Dieting Too Far," by Renu George, *New Youth Connections*, November 1996

"What Are Eating Disorders?" by Stephanie Perez, *New Youth Connections*, December 2004

"Starving for Acceptance," by Anonymous, *New Youth Connections*, December 2004

"Male on the Scale," by Anonymous, *New Youth Connections*, May/June 2000

"My Secret Habit," by Anonymous, *New Youth Connections*, September/October 1992

"Traumatized by Eating," by Autumn Bush, *Represent*, September/October 2000

"Skinniest Man in the Graveyard," by Anonymous, *New Youth Connections*, March 2008

"Sticks and Stones," by Anne Ueland, *Represent*, September/October, 2003

"Finding My Way Home," by Aquellah Mahdi, *Represent*, November/December 2007

"Recovering From An Eating Disorder," *Represent*, November/December 2007

About Youth Communication

Youth Communication, founded in 1980, is a nonprofit youth development program located in New York City whose mission is to teach writing, journalism, and leadership skills. The teenagers we train become writers for our websites and books and for two print magazines, *New Youth Connections*, a general-interest youth magazine, and *Represent*, a magazine by and for young people in foster care.

Each year, up to 100 young people participate in Youth Communication's school-year and summer journalism workshops where they work under the direction of full-time professional editors. Most are African American, Latino, or Asian, and many are recent immigrants. The opportunity to reach their peers with accurate portrayals of their lives and important self-help information motivates the young writers to create powerful stories.

Our goal is to run a strong youth development program in which teens produce high quality stories that inform and inspire their peers. Doing so requires us to be sensitive to the complicated lives and emotions of the teen participants while also providing an intellectually rigorous experience. We achieve that goal in the writing/teaching/editing relationship, which is the core of our program.

Our teaching and editorial process begins with discussions

between adult editors and the teen staff. In those meetings, the teens and the editors work together to identify the most important issues in the teens' lives and to figure out how those issues can be turned into stories that will resonate with teen readers.

Once story topics are chosen, students begin the process of crafting their stories. For a personal story, that means revisiting events in one's past to understand their significance for the future. For a commentary, it means developing a logical and persuasive point of view. For a reported story, it means gathering information through research and interviews. Students look inward and outward as they try to make sense of their experiences and the world around them and find the points of intersection between personal and social concerns. That process can take a few weeks or a few months. Stories frequently go through ten or more drafts as students work under the guidance of their editors, the way any professional writer does.

Many of the students who walk through our doors have uneven skills, as a result of poor education, living under extremely stressful conditions, or coming from homes where English is a second language. Yet, to complete their stories, students must successfully perform a wide range of activities, including writing and rewriting, reading, discussion, reflection, research, interviewing, and typing. They must work as members of a team and they must accept individual responsibility. They learn to provide constructive criticism, and to accept it. They engage in explorations of truthfulness, fairness, and accuracy. They meet deadlines. They must develop the audacity to believe that they have something important to say and the humility to recognize that saying it well is not a process of instant gratification. Rather, it usually requires a long, hard struggle through many discussions and much rewriting.

It would be impossible to teach these skills and dispositions as separate, disconnected topics, like grammar, ethics, or assertiveness. However, we find that students make rapid progress when they are learning skills in the context of an inquiry that is personally significant to them and that will benefit their peers.

When teens publish their stories—in *New Youth Connections* and *Represent*, on the web, and in other publications—they reach tens of thousands of teen and adult readers. Teachers, counselors, social workers, and other adults circulate the stories to young people in their classes and out-of-school youth programs. Adults tell us that teens in their programs—including many who are ordinarily resistant to reading—clamor for the stories. Teen readers report that the stories give them information they can't get anywhere else, and inspire them to reflect on their lives and open lines of communication with adults.

Writers usually participate in our program for one semester, though some stay much longer. Years later, many of them report that working here was a turning point in their lives—that it helped them acquire the confidence and skills that they needed for success in college and careers. Scores of our graduates have overcome tremendous obstacles to become journalists, writers, and novelists. They include National Book Award finalist Edwidge Danticat, novelist Ernesto Quinonez, writer Veronica Chambers and *New York Times* reporter Rachel Swarns. Hundreds more are working in law, business, and other careers. Many are teachers, principals, and youth workers, and several have started nonprofit youth programs themselves and work as mentors—helping another generation of young people develop their skills and find their voices.

Youth Communication is a nonprofit educational corporation. Contributions are gratefully accepted and are tax deductible to the fullest extent of the law.

To make a contribution, or for information about our publications and programs, including our catalog of over 100 books and curricula for hard-to-reach teens, see www.youthcomm.org

About The Editors

Hope Vanderberg was the editor of *New Youth Connections*, Youth Communication's magazine by and for New York City teens, from 2004 to 2008.

Prior to working at Youth Communication, Vanderberg specialized in science journalism and environmental education. She was an editor at Medscape.com, a medical website, wrote articles for *Audubon* and *The Sciences* magazines, and taught children and teens at environmental education centers in California and Texas. She has also worked as a field biologist, studying bird behavior in Puerto Rico.

She has a master's degree in science and environmental journalism from New York University and a bachelor's degree from Earlham College. She is currently a freelance editor.

Keith Hefner co-founded Youth Communication in 1980 and has directed it ever since. He is the recipient of the Luther P. Jackson Education Award from the New York Association of Black Journalists and a MacArthur Fellowship. He was also a Revson Fellow at Columbia University.

Laura Longhine is the editorial director at Youth Communication. She edited *Represent*, Youth Communication's magazine by and for youth in foster care, for three years, and has written for a variety of publications. She has a BA in English from Tufts University and an MS in Journalism from Columbia University.

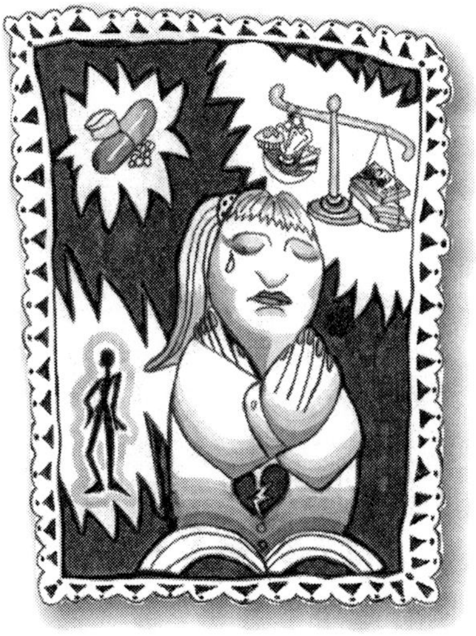

More Helpful Books From Youth Comunication

The Struggle to Be Strong: True Stories by Teens About Overcoming Tough Times. Foreword by Veronica Chambers. Help young people identify and build on their own strengths with 30 personal stories about resiliency. (Free Spirit)

Starting With "I": Personal Stories by Teenagers. "Who am I and who do I want to become?" Thirty-five stories examine this question through the lenses of race, ethnicity, gender, sexuality, family, and more. Increase this book's value with the free Teacher's Guide, available from youthcomm.org. (Youth Communication)

Real Stories, Real Teens. Inspire teens to read and recognize their strengths with this collection of 26 true stories by teens. The young writers describe how they overcame significant challenges and stayed true to themselves. Also includes the first chapters from three novels in the Bluford Series. (Youth Communication)

The Courage to Be Yourself: True Stories by Teens About Cliques, Conflicts, and Overcoming Peer Pressure. In 26 first-person stories, teens write about their lives with searing honesty. These stories will inspire young readers to reflect on their own lives, work through their problems, and help them discover who they really are. (Free Spirit)

Out With It: Gay and Straight Teens Write About Homosexuality. Break stereotypes and provide support with this unflinching look at gay life from a teen's perspective. With a focus on urban youth, this book also includes several heterosexual teens' transformative experiences with gay peers. (Youth Communication)

Things Get Hectic: Teens Write About the Violence That Surrounds Them. Violence is commonplace in many teens' lives, be it bullying, gangs, dating, or family relationships. Hear the experiences of victims, perpetrators, and witnesses through more than 50 real-world stories. (Youth Communication)

From Dropout to Achiever: Teens Write About School. Help teens overcome the challenges of graduating, which may involve overcoming family problems, bouncing back from a bad semester, or dropping out for a time. These teens show how they achieve academic success. (Youth Communication)

My Secret Addiction: Teens Write About Cutting. These true accounts of cutting, or self-mutilation, offer a window into the personal and family situations that lead to this secret habit, and show how teens can get the help they need. (Youth Communication)

Sticks and Stones: Teens Write About Bullying. Shed light on bullying, as told from the perspectives of the perpetrator, the victim, and the witness. These stories show why bullying occurs, the harm it causes, and how it might be prevented. (Youth Communication)

Boys to Men: Teens Write About Becoming a Man. The young men in this book write about their confusion, ideals, and the challenges of becoming a man. Their honesty and courage make them role models for teens who are bombarded with contradictory messages about what it means to be a man. (Youth Communication)

To order these and other books, go to:
www.youthcomm.org
or call 212-279-0708 x115